Remaking Culture on Wall Street

Henry Engler

Remaking Culture on Wall Street

A Behavioral Science Approach for Building Trust from the Bottom Up

Henry Engler
Thomson Reuters
Regulatory Intelligence
New York, NY, USA

ISBN 978-3-030-02085-9   ISBN 978-3-030-02086-6   (eBook)
https://doi.org/10.1007/978-3-030-02086-6

Library of Congress Control Number: 2018959737

© The Editor(s) (if applicable) and The Author(s), under exclusive license to Springer Nature Switzerland AG 2018
This work is subject to copyright. All rights are solely and exclusively licensed by the Publisher, whether the whole or part of the material is concerned, specifically the rights of translation, reprinting, reuse of illustrations, recitation, broadcasting, reproduction on microfilms or in any other physical way, and transmission or information storage and retrieval, electronic adaptation, computer software, or by similar or dissimilar methodology now known or hereafter developed.
The use of general descriptive names, registered names, trademarks, service marks, etc. in this publication does not imply, even in the absence of a specific statement, that such names are exempt from the relevant protective laws and regulations and therefore free for general use.
The publisher, the authors and the editors are safe to assume that the advice and information in this book are believed to be true and accurate at the date of publication. Neither the publisher nor the authors or the editors give a warranty, express or implied, with respect to the material contained herein or for any errors or omissions that may have been made. The publisher remains neutral with regard to jurisdictional claims in published maps and institutional affiliations.

Cover image: © Oleg Korshakov/Moment/Getty
Author Photo by Alistair Duncan

This Palgrave Macmillan imprint is published by the registered company Springer Nature Switzerland AG
The registered company address is: Gewerbestrasse 11, 6330 Cham, Switzerland

Acknowledgements

There is a lot to go around. First, the book would not be possible were it not for the opportunity afforded to me by Thomson Reuters to write about financial regulation and the problems of conduct and culture over the past five years. To that end, special thanks to my editor Randall Mikkelsen, and our global editor, Alexander Robson, both of whom who provided support, encouragement and the flexibility to complete the project. Other colleagues at Thomson Reuters include Dave Curran, Mark Harrop, and Alex Ferrill, for helping to shape our public forums and roundtable events. These were tremendous learning experiences, and great opportunities to bring together industry leaders, regulators, and experts in the field.

On the receiving end, Tula Weiss and Jacqueline Young at Palgrave Macmillan have been terrific to work with. Their patience and guidance through the publishing process have been invaluable. I'm very grateful for all their hard work.

In the academic word, a special thanks to Malcolm Salter at the Harvard Business School. Our numerous conversations on culture in financial services, particularly at the early stage of my thinking, helped to form a foundation that led to the project. Also, thanks to Eugene Soltes at HBS for providing his own thoughts on what drives otherwise good people to do bad things in financial services.

The book would not have seen the light of day were it not for the generous support and help of many at the Federal Reserve Bank of New York, in particular, Bill Dudley, who kindly provided time for a lengthy interview on these issues. His insights and steadfast commitment to reforming culture have been an inspiration to further the cause. Also, many thanks to Michael

Held, Tom Noone, James Hennessy, Jack Gutt, and Andrea Priest for their support and help to facilitate conversations. A great debt of gratitude goes to Thomas Baxter who, while at the New York Fed, joined our initial conferences on culture, giving our clients his insights into a complex issue.

In thinking through how to take the concepts of behavioral science and apply them to conduct and cultural issues at banks, the Dutch National Bank has been at the forefront of this effort. My conversations with Wijnand Nuits at the DNB helped to further my understanding how behavioral science can be applied in bank supervision. His willingness to help and provide additional information on the DNB's philosophy is truly welcome. Lengthy conversations with Mirea Raaijmakers, a former DNB supervisor, as well as Wieke Scholtens and Shweta Pajpani at RBS in London, provided the book with the nuts and bolts of how to operationalize behavioral science. Many thanks to all of you in helping shape my thinking and recommendations.

There are others in the industry who deserve thanks for their interest and support. They include Azish Filabi, Una Neary, P. J. Dearden, Sally Dewar, Henry Kaufman, Stephen Scott and Steven Mandis. In addition, many thanks to Moritz Romer of the DNB, Orlando Fernández Ruiz of the Bank of England and Mikael Down of the Banking Standards Board for their recent participation in our public forums.

Regarding the writing process, thanks to Kevin Lennon, who made the early mornings on the 8th floor of NYU's Bobst library more bearable through his humor and banter. Thanks also to the librarians at Fairfield University's DiMenna-Nyselius library for the early morning greetings while unlocking doors.

Finally, a tremendous thanks to Regina, Marina, and Matthew for putting up with all of this and listening to my endless stories, many of which I no doubt repeated several times. And lastly, to my dad, Henry. Your never-ending interest, support and energy are an inspiration to us all.

September 2018 Henry Engler

Contents

1 Introduction   1

2 The Financial Crisis: The Culture Problem Emerges   7

3 Culture and Organizational Size   37

4 Global Regulators: Limits on What They Can Do   47

5 Enforcing Culture: Criminally Based Compliance   59

6 Behavioral Science: From Theory to Practice   67

7 U.S. Regulators: Requiring Behavioral Risk Teams   85

8 What Is Finance For?   93

Index   99

1

Introduction

In the early months of 1980, Ivan Boesky & Company, a Wall Street risk arbitrage firm, offered me a job. I was in my senior year at NYU's College of Business and Public Administration with only a few months to go before graduation. My major was economics, and to secure a job after graduation, I began applying to various financial firms. Boesky & Company responded to my overture and invited me to their offices at 77 Water Street in downtown Manhattan in early February. I was ecstatic. I had followed Boesky closely and became intrigued with the practice of risk arbitrage, essentially the purchase or sale of securities that are considered mispriced, often because of some looming change in a company's ownership or structure, and which usually manifests itself in the form of a takeover. Boesky was one of the Street's most successful arbitrageurs, who along with Robert Rubin at Goldman Sachs, Guy Weyser-Pratte at Pru-Bache, and Richard Rosenthal at Salomon Brothers became known as the "Four Horsemen" of Wall Street. It was a lucrative business, but what attracted me most was the opaque nature of risk arbitrage and what would appear to be a combination of intellect, timing and chance. Boesky and his competitors were the masters of this arcane corner of finance, deftly placing and removing their bets just at the right time to reap enormous profits. The skill that lay behind this practice filled me with both awe and curiosity.

When I applied to Boesky's firm I had little hope that they would respond. It was a long shot in my view, but one worth taking, and as a 21-year old from Brooklyn I reckoned I had nothing to lose. When I arrived at their Water Street office on a blustery February morning, I was ushered into a tastefully decorated office, with forest green wallpaper, gold-framed paintings of pastoral landscapes, and antique-looking furniture that echoed a distant period in finance. The room was bathed in a soft glow from several lamps stationed in various parts of the room. In the center was a well-polished wooden desk, with curved legs and no draws or cabinets below. It could have easily been sitting in someone's study on upper Park Avenue. It was a desk for reading, thought and contemplation, or writing letters longhand to distant relatives abroad. It was far removed from any trading room on Wall Street. The whole setting gave me the sense of polish, seriousness, and probity.

After a few minutes a gentleman of around 40 years walked into the room and introduced himself. His title and name now escape me, but behind his horn-rimmed glasses, receding hairline and expensive shirt and tie, emerged what at the time I could only describe as a WASPish type of character, one that I had rarely come across as a youth growing up in New York City, but now realized that through the various canyons of Wall Street I would run into such polished and urbane individuals quite frequently. He spoke in a direct, yet soft manner, without any discernible regional accent. He had a serious demeanor about him as he reviewed my resume. When he looked up he asked a few questions about what I wanted to do in the future, and after replying something along the lines of wanting to apply my NYU degree to better understanding financial markets, he said: "I'd like to offer you a position." Just what that position was I also don't now recall, but what I do remember is being startled beyond belief. The thought that I might go to work for Ivan Boesky was beyond the realm of my reality. It was as though I had hit the jackpot. I was elated, and the thought of coming to work every day after graduation at this storied firm was more than I could have hoped for. There was just one catch. "We need you to start now," said the bespectacled financier in his calm and cool manner. "Start now?" I asked. "Yes. We can really use someone like you right away." I can now imagine the look on my face was probably one of confusion mixed with anxiety, and after gathering my composure I asked whether I might have some time to think about it. The answer was I had until tomorrow.

Riding home on the subway after the interview I found myself confused and depressed. Why now? What could be so urgent? Couldn't they wait a few months until I graduate? Why the rush! It was a devil's bargain, I thought. Perhaps they were testing me, trying to see how much I wanted it; the cut and thrust of risk arbitrage at one of the top firms on the Street. Anyone else would jump at the chance. School? Graduation? That could wait, others might say. A job offer from Boesky? Where do I sign?

When I arrived home I told my parents about what just had happened. A puzzled look also came over their faces. But your education? Do you want to throw it all away? Of course not. They had sacrificed a lot to send to me to NYU, which even at that time was not a cheap place to get an education. I had done well and enjoyed my studies. I had come across a wide range of professors, from Marxists to free-traders to the Austrian school of economics. I was ready for the real world, so I thought, but not for this. Not for a decision where I had to weigh the risks carefully on both sides.

I turned down Boesky's offer, and within a few months of graduation I landed a job as a research assistant in the economics department of Chemical Bank, which at the time stood on the other side of the Chase Manhattan Plaza from the Federal Reserve Bank of New York. During the job interview the clincher seemed to be when I said I admired the writings of Friedrich von Hayek and his strong anti-socialist views; how society must be free to arrange itself lest it avoid the slippery slope of excessive government intervention. Little did I know that my interviewer was an economist who adored Hayek; a political conservative who was only too happy to offer this young man a job.

The following 12 years were some of my most enjoyable in the financial industry. I had great mentors who taught me how to understand monetary policy and the workings of the U.S. economy. I advanced quickly to a senior economist role, and by the age of 28 I was on the bank's trading floor explaining the actions of the Federal Reserve in the open market to traders, salespeople and their clients. It was an exciting time, particularly given that one had to interpret the Fed's actions in the U.S. government securities market in order to understand whether they were easing or tightening monetary policy. The most challenging and frightening point during that period was the stock market crash in October 1987. No one knew what to expect following the dramatic 508-point plunge of the Dow Industrials. All we could tell our traders and clients is that the Fed had to open the monetary floodgates. It did, and what many of us thought would be the onset of a major depression was averted. Yet, around the same time something else happened that opened my eyes to the workings of the real world.

Timothy Tabor was a star trader on Wall Street, working at Kidder Peabody, when Chemical Bank decided to hire him in 1986. He was a risk arbitrageur, a business the bank decided it wanted to get into. When Tabor, a tall, lean, good-looking guy arrived on the trading floor he ingratiated himself to all the female staffers by having a bouquet of red roses delivered to each of them. Many of us didn't know what to make of this grand gesture, but the women loved it. He had a certain star power. He was different.

He came from an unfamiliar part of Wall Street, one more mysterious and lucrative than the traditional markets in which the bank operated. But after a while someone senior on the bank's board decided that risk arbitrage was too risky a business. It wasn't clear to me at the time whether Tabor had lost money, but for whatever reason both he and Chemical Bank parted ways. Some months thereafter the front page of the *New York Times* announced that U.S. Federal agents had arrested Tabor at his Manhattan apartment. He was charged with insider trading while working at Kidder Peabody. But Tabor wasn't the only one implicated. On that snowy morning of February 12, 1987, Robert Freeman, a partner at Goldman Sachs, who worked under Robert Rubin in the risk arbitrage unit, was arrested on the firm's trading floor by U.S. agents. He was also charged with insider trading. A third individual, Richard B. Wigton, a colleague of Tabor's, was also arrested that morning. The arrests sent shockwaves through Wall Street, casting a pall over the industry, most notably at Goldman, which was widely revered and at the time still privately held. What followed was a series of events that led to one of the biggest scandals in the industry's history. In December 1987, Ivan Boesky, one of Wall Street's most powerful speculators, was sentenced to three years in prison for conspiring to file false stock trading records. The lucrative gains made by Boesky were fueled by inside information over when various companies would merge or buy out others. The charges exposed what had been a secret web of traders, with Boesky at the helm, dealing off of proprietary information and reaping enormous profits. At his sentencing, Federal District Judge Morris E. Lasker said: "Ivan Boesky's offense cannot go unpunished. Its scope was too great, its influence too profound, its seriousness too substantial merely to forgive and forget."[1]

The Boesky scandal affected me in two ways. First, it removed the blinders I had as a young industry professional about how business was done in certain areas. It demonstrated that what at first glance might appear to be superior knowledge and expertise was actually fraud, fueled by excessive greed and a willingness to break the law. This was the first time I and many other young professionals had witnessed such behavior, but as we all know, it wouldn't be the last. The Boesky affair seemed to be an anomaly—a secret cabal of a few insiders who worked in a business that few outsiders understood. But the second impression I had brought me back to 77 Water Street and the job offer from Boesky & Company in 1980. At the time, I was deeply torn and conflicted, but decided to decline the offer and finish my studies. What I didn't know at the time was that I made a decision informed by my aversion to risk, the type of thinking that many of us go through when confronted with choices that affect our material or financial well-being. Behavioral economics calls this "loss aversion," and work in this area has been led by Amos Tversky and Daniel Kahneman, with the latter winning a Nobel Prize in economics in 2002 for his research. Loss aversion theory acknowledges that for many individuals "losses loom larger than gains"; that the pain of losing is psychologically about twice as powerful as the pleasure of gaining. The influence of behavioral economics has grown steadily, with Richard Thaler at the University of Chicago Booth School of Business, taking home the Nobel in 2017. Thaler's most recent book, "Misbehaving: The Making of Behavioral Economics,"[2] takes us through the origins of this new and innovative approach toward economics, one that has not always found favor with mainstream economists. What behavioral science tries to do is understand what motivates individuals to make decisions, even if at times when those decisions don't seem to be in their best interest. Within the financial industry what we have seen since the 2008 financial crisis are numerous instances of people "misbehaving." The costs to the industry, both financial and reputational have been considerable, and the behaviors uncovered range from the individual, "rogue" trader to groups of people both within and outside firms colluding with one another to manipulate markets in foreign exchange and Libor pricing, for example. The sheer extent of the misconduct has led U.S. and foreign regulators to intervene and warn firms to get their houses in order and put a stop to the misconduct. Banks have responded in numerous ways, including the development of what one might call a "surveillance state," where employees are monitored in ways that Orwell would never have imagined. These "criminally-based" compliance programs, many led by former enforcement officials hired from regulatory agencies, may be able to have some deterrent effect on misbehavior, but in numerous interviews and discussions over the past few years with banking executives and regulators, it's clear that the industry is not where it wants to be on these issues. It's because of this lack of progress that some are turning to behavioral science to get at the root causes of such behavior, attempting to understand what drives good people to do bad things.

In this book we will examine several of the most prominent scandals over the past decade and speculate how they came about, what were the drivers behind them, and why such behavior flourished for considerable lengths of time. We will outline the regulatory response to the scandals, what has been proposed and what might be in the offing should misconduct persist. Lastly, we will examine whether behavioral science can provide companies with tools that better enable them to identify circumstances when employees are tempted to cross the line. For example, are we able to identify common elements that give rise to such behavior? By doing so we should also be able to frame the hallmarks of a strong corporate culture, one that allows employees to flourish in an environment where they are trusted.

This book will not have all the answers. This is merely a first step toward understanding alternative methods and techniques that might assist the management of financial institutions in restoring trust and ethics in their organizations. It is critical that they do so ahead of the next crisis, when they might not have the luxury of acting on their own.

Notes

1. "Boesky Sentenced to 3 Years in Jail in Insider Scandal," James Sterngold, *The New York Times*, December 19, 1987.
2. *Misbehaving: The Making of Behavioral Economics*, Richard Thaler, W. W. Norton & Company, Inc., 2015.

2

The Financial Crisis: The Culture Problem Emerges

Trading rooms are a world unto themselves when it comes to workplace environments. Within large financial organizations they are distinct from other parts of the business, not only by the nature of what they do, which often incorporates degrees of risk and leverage well beyond the limits of other businesses, but also by the individuals who run such operations, and those attracted to them. The inhabitants of these vast football fields of red and green blinking computer screens once came from mostly lower and middle-income origins. They were often young men who had an affinity with numbers, a gift of banter, and an almost innate skill at playing the odds. They were gamblers, and in their free time would as easily place a bet on the fifth race at Pimlico as they would wager on whether pound sterling would open higher in Asian trading the next morning. In the UK, young traders in the City used to be called "barrow boys," a nineteenth-century reference to street traders who sold goods, such as fish and vegetables, from two-wheeled barrows. In London's banks, such young lads, often hired without a college degree, were looked down upon by upper class merchant bankers. But when it came to dealing with foreign exchange, stocks or bonds, the skills of these boys became apparent, reaping large profits for their employers while having fun doing it. They were in their element, and it was all legitimate.

Of course, more recently, the entry requirements to trading rooms have changed. Now, an MBA is required. Across various markets trading has become more technical, and high-level quantitative skills are in greater demand, especially with the growth of derivatives, where sophisticated models and algorithms

© The Author(s) 2018
H. Engler, *Remaking Culture on Wall Street*,
https://doi.org/10.1007/978-3-030-02086-6_2

have become more the norm rather than spot trading in the U.S. dollar or Treasury two-year note. Machines have steadily replaced humans in executing so-called "plain vanilla" transactions. While the human element is not what it once was in over-the-counter (OTC) markets such as foreign exchange, it has not disappeared entirely. The trading units at large banks are now smaller than they used to be, but the makeup and character of the individuals sitting behind those multi-colored screens are still different from those in other parts of the institution. The lure and attraction of trading is still present, offering the prospect of large salaries and even larger bonuses. The ebb and flow of markets, the satisfaction of being positioned correctly for a large price swing, all this still brings about an inner joy from those who have that gaming streak in them.

Two of the largest scandals to emerge in the post-crisis period involved markets where the trading floor was at the heart of what went wrong: the foreign exchange and Libor rate-fixing scandals. Both scandals included a multitude of banks who colluded on pricing to the detriment of their customers. Much has been written about them, and there is no desire to go over the same ground, particularly the intricate and technical details of the price collusion. Instead, what we will focus on are the individuals involved in these episodes, the small world they inhabited, the language they used, and, hopefully, discern some insights into why they behaved the way they did.

Following this review, we'll then look at two other high-profile scandals, both different in nature, yet perhaps similar in the motivations of the principal actors involved: the Goldman Sachs subprime mortgage product case where a relatively low-level employee, Fabrice Tourre, served jail time and paid a substantial fine for defrauding investors in a subprime mortgage product that failed during the financial crisis. Lastly, we will examine the more recent Wells Fargo fraudulent account opening case, where more than three million fake retail accounts and credit cards were opened up by the bank, costing millions in restitution to its customers.

Foreign Exchange: The Last Frontier

The foreign exchange market is the world's largest and most actively traded financial market. According to numbers provided by Bank for International Settlements in its most recent Triennial Central Bank Survey, FX markets averaged $5.1 trillion per day in April 2016.[1] In the 2015 U.S. District Court complaint against the 13 banks alleged to have fixed the benchmark prices of currencies in the market, it was estimated that the group had a combined market share of over 90%.[2]

The FX market is also the least regulated when compared to global equities, bonds, or other markets. It is largely an OTC market, and as outlined in the complaint, the "United States does not have any specific rules or agencies governing FX spot, outright forward, or FX swap transactions." There is no centralized exchange that collects and posts real-time trade information for the market. And while the banks' proprietary trading systems allow them to match buyers with sellers, real-time order flow and volume data is not available to the market. The banks "closely guard their real-time order flow and volume data from the public and do not make it commercially available for purchase." As the complaint notes, the relative opaqueness of the market "substantially limits knowledge of traders' conduct inside these dealing platforms and on the voice trading desk."

What is described in the 187-page U.S. Federal complaint is a self-contained network of traders who run the biggest financial market in the world, relatively untouched by regulatory constraints or oversight. In terms of the actual number of individuals involved in the alleged collusion, the group was described as "small and close-knit," having "formed strong ties by working with one another in prior trading positions." Many of the traders also lived near each other, in the same neighborhoods in the Essex countryside just northeast of London's financial district. They also belonged to the same social clubs, golfed together, dined together, and sat on many of the same charity boards. As Andre Spicer, a professor at the Cass Business School in London, said, "[T]he foreign-exchange market has a very strong culture, in which practitioners feel more attached to each other than they do their banks."[3]

So far, we get the picture of a group of individuals who know each other very well, share the same interests, live in the same neighborhoods and have powerful roles in overseeing the same business at their respective firms. One of the fundamental tenets of behavioral science is that humans have biases; that unlike the rational, optimizing agents described by neoclassical economic theory, the decision-making process of individuals can be influenced by factors that defy understanding. Biases are a part of life. We all have them, and they often remain with us for very long periods of time. How we acquire those biases can vary. They can come from many corners of our lives; those we associate with, whether family, friends, or work colleagues, can help shape and mold our biases. In what we've learned so far about the individuals who once ran the world's largest financial market, it may be safe to assume that they shared many common beliefs, attitudes and, even biases. There is also a tendency among individuals who work in small groups to conform to the norms of that group, even if they initially might feel at odds with some of the behaviors displayed. As Thaler and Sunstein note: "People become more likely to conform when they know that other people will see what they have to say. Sometimes people will go along with the group even when they think, or know, that everyone else has blundered. Unanimous groups are able to provide the strongest nudges – even when the question is an easy one, and people ought to know that everyone else is wrong."[4] The tendency for individuals to accept what the group says as correct, legitimate, and in certain cases, legal, is a powerful force, and one that we will come back to as we analyze other episodes of misconduct.

When the FX traders communicated with each other, they used chat rooms, the documentation of which served as the smoking-gun behind the allegations of price collusion on currencies. The chat rooms had names, including: "The Cartel," "The Bandits' Club," "The Mafia," and "One Team, One Dream." Other chat rooms described themselves as "The Sterling Lads," "The Players," "The 3 Musketeers," "A Co-operative," and "The A-team." The names of the chat rooms speak volumes in terms of the objectives of the members. Membership of certain chat rooms was by invitation only, suggesting that future members went through some sort of a vetting process before being invited, much like other private clubs one might think of. We can only speculate on how individuals were chosen—there doesn't appear to be any record of the actual process—but from what has been described it seems that new members were evaluated on what they could contribute to the club and gauged against the same personal characteristics of those already on the inside, including their views, opinions, and biases.

According to a consent order from the New York State Department of Financial Services (NYDFS), "One Barclays FX trader, when he became the main Euro trader for Barclays in 2011, was desperate to be invited to join the Cartel because of the trading advantages from sharing information with the other main traders of the Euro. After extensive discussion of whether or not this trader 'would add value' to the Cartel, he was invited to join for a '1 month trial,' but was advised 'mess this up and sleep with one eye open at night.' This trader ultimately survived his 'trial' and was permitted to remain in the Cartel chat room until it was disbanded at some point in 2012."[5]

What emerges from some of the transcripts of the chat rooms further underscores the sense of shared purpose and notion of helping one another achieve a desired outcome. As one Barclays trader stated on a multi-bank chat: "we 5 are 3 of the top 4 eur books on the planet … if we cant help each other with liquidity … who can?" (The reference to "eur" is the Euro currency.) In another chat in December 2011, a Barclays trader told another at Citigroup: "If u bigger. He will step out of the way…We gonna help u."

2 The Financial Crisis: The Culture Problem Emerges

While much of the collusive behavior occurred among the top traders at each bank for the currencies they were responsible for. The practice of defrauding customers also spread to the sales team, who engaged directly with the bank's clients. At Barclays, for example, sales staff engaged in "hard mark-ups" of the price of currencies quoted to a client. A hard mark-up represents the difference between the price the trader gives a salesperson and the price the salesperson shows to the client. According to NYDFS documents, "FX Sales employees would determine the appropriate mark-up by calculating the most advantageous rate for Barclays that did not cause the client to question whether executing the transaction with the Bank was a good idea, based on the relationship with the client, recent pricing history, client expectations and other factors." The sales staff also sat near the traders, often allowing them to communicate verbally or "through the use of hand signals."

The level of mark-up was determined by calculating the best rate for Barclays, and the price quoted to the customer, including mark-up, would have to appear competitive to the client. One Barclays salesperson wrote in a chat to an employee at another bank in December 2009: "hard mark up is key... but i was taught early...u dont have clients...u dont make money...so dont be stupid."

In one of the more damning quotes prosecutors used to show the clear intent of defrauding clients, a Barclays' vice president in New York (who later became co-head of UK FX hedge fund sales) wrote in a November 2010 chat: "markup is making sure you make the right decision on price...which is whats the worst price i can put on this where the customers decision to trade with me or give me future business doesn't change...if you aint cheating, you aint trying."

One of the more astonishing aspects of this case—and in others, as we will see—is how long such collusive behavior flourished. These were not one-off events, but rather orchestrated and coordinated manipulation of critical benchmark prices for many years. In the FX case, the allegations are that the banks colluded for at least a decade. As noted earlier, the global foreign exchange market is perhaps the least regulated among the primary financial markets. What that means is that both external oversight of the market from domestic and international regulators, and internal surveillance and oversight within the banks implicated was severely lacking for the collusion to have lasted so long.

What the length of time also underscores is that fraudulent behavior became the norm or accepted rules of engagement with bank customers. During a 10-year period, traders and salespeople come and go. Some leave to join other banks, and in this case those banks would have likely been involved in the collusion. Others leave the industry entirely. Still others, new recruits, fresh from university, enter the dealing room and find themselves confronted with behavior that they find at odds with their ethics and conscience. The choices they have are clear: find some alternative form of employment, or swallow your conscience and accept that this is the way the world works. If they choose the latter, they become party to a system in which the behavioral norms of the group overpower those of the individual, a pattern that behavioral scientists would find only too familiar.

What have we learned about the inner workings of the FX trading groups during this period; their culture, and who knew what and when?

Perry Stimpson was a forex trader at Citibank until he was fired in November 2014, after evidence emerged that he shared confidential client information with other banks by using "chat rooms," or electronic messaging platforms. Stimpson responded by taking the bank to a London employee tribunal, claiming unfair dismissal.[6]

"Now in the glare of scrutiny from regulators these activities look wrong," Stimpson said in 2015 under cross-examination during the tribunal. "But at the time they were market convention," Stimpson told the court, and explained how senior forex staff shared information about client activities, and that senior management condoned the activity as they were aware of it but took no action. "If you look at any organization, surely you look to senior management," Stimpson said. "The culture in any organization is set by senior management down. If you see senior management do something, it implies to you it's OK." Citibank responded to Stimpson's accusations by saying: "Mr. Stimpson is making these allegations to deflect attention from his own misconduct. All of the allegations of wrongdoing being made by Mr Stimpson have been investigated and were found to be without merit."

While Stimpson admitted he shared information about a central bank client in a chat room, he said whether client information could be shared was a "bit of a gray area." Citibank staff knew that details of some client activities were strictly confidential, but the actions of central banks were widely shared, he said. "It was implicitly understood that central banks were OK to talk about … It was standard market practice that went on for years," he said. Citibank told the tribunal it had concerns that Stimpson breached client confidentiality on at least 12 occasions in chat room conversations, which broke its code of conduct. Citibank said its code of conduct made no exceptions for central banks or any clients. Stimpson agreed, but said the bank did not provide guidelines on what was allowed in chat rooms until January 2013. The bank's lawyer, Diya Sen Gupta, said because other traders shared information in chat rooms did not allow Stimpson to do so. "Just because other people are doing something wrong, doesn't mean you are excused from your own behavior." In the end, the tribunal accepted Stimpson's argument that Citibank took a very narrow approach, relying on the written code of its policies without observing what occurred in practice. The tribunal found it was reasonable for Stimpson to behave the way he did given the culture of information sharing and how his colleagues behaved in practice.

As behavioral scientists and psychologists have shown, people are often challenged to do the right thing when everyone else around them seems to believe that their bad behavior is perfectly fine. Moreover, when a certain way of doing things becomes the norm, it can remain that way for prolonged periods of time, this despite the emergence of new entrants or individuals who initially might not agree with the group's decision-making process. The process is known as "collective conservatism," the tendency of groups to stick to established patterns even as new needs arise.

Perry Stimpson was not the only trader to challenge what he believed was behavior that went along with the approved norms of the group. Carly McWilliams, a trader in the same Citibank FX unit, also challenged her dismissal in court, highlighting what for her was standard business practice.

"My dismissal is overwhelmingly harsh and inappropriate, given that the alleged offenses were nothing other than normal practices of my everyday job at the time, that were encouraged, condoned, required and indeed rewarded by management," McWilliams told the tribunal.[7] "The Bank has encouraged precisely what it now complains of. I did not invent our practices. That is what I was introduced to and what has operated since I was introduced to it," said McWilliams. "It is what I was required to do." McWilliams, along with Stimpson, and two other Citibank traders won their tribunal cases of wrongful dismissal, with all of them claiming in one form or another that their behavior was in line with what management deemed appropriate at the time.

Libor Rate Rigging: No Room for Morals

When do we know that something we are doing is wrong? Do we know it instinctively, or is it learned over time through our associations with others? When examining the behavior of key actors in the Libor trading scandal, described by some as the greatest financial scandal ever, one can begin to question where personal morals begin, and where they end; how one might start off believing in one set of standards or morals, and later find that they clash with those who you spend most of your waking hours with.

The Libor (London Interbank Offered Rate) scandal involved the manipulation of one of the global economy's most important interest-rate benchmarks. The rate is used to determine payments on about $800 trillion-worth of financial instruments, ranging from complex interest-rate derivatives to simple mortgages. It is a critical linchpin to global capital flows, and from about 2000 to 2009 the rate was manipulated by traders to enhance their profits on trading positions.

The setting of the Libor rate was in many ways a throwback to a time when the City of London was a clubby environment. Everyone knew each other. They lunched and dined together, entertained the same clients, joined the same clubs. Trust was more important than a legal contract. During the period under review, and for decades before, the Libor borrowing rate was set daily by a panel of banks for ten currencies and 15 maturities. The most important of these, three-month dollar Libor, indicated what a bank would pay to borrow dollars for three months from other banks at 11 am on the day it was set. It was in many ways a reflection of the bank's funding needs. The dollar rate was fixed each day by taking estimates from a panel, at the time comprised of 18 banks. The rates they submitted reflected what they believed they would have to pay to borrow if they needed money. The top four and bottom four estimates were discarded, and the actual Libor rate is the average of those left. The submissions of all the participants are published, along with each day's Libor fix, and then used around the world to set payments on a broad range of diverse financial instruments and contracts.

(Libor was previously published by the British Bankers Association. Libor rates are now calculated by London's Intercontinental Exchange (ICE), and published by Thomson Reuters. The new Libor rates along various maturities are referred to as ICE LIBOR, and are calculated under a new methodology. ICE defines Libor as "[a] wholesale funding rate anchored in LIBOR panel banks' unsecured wholesale transactions to the greatest extent possible, with a waterfall to enable a rate to be published in all market circumstances." The Waterfall Methodology requires LIBOR panel banks to base their submissions in eligible wholesale, unsecured funding transactions to the extent available, and was implemented after the rate-rigging scandal. Alternatives to LIBOR are being investigated, with the Federal Reserve Bank of New York having convened the Alternative Reference Rate Committee in 2014.)[8]

2 The Financial Crisis: The Culture Problem Emerges   15

For as many years as this practice took place, it was assumed that the interest rates emerging from the daily process were a truthful reflection of what banks would be willing to pay to borrow money. Given the relatively small size of the market, everyone was also aware of what others were doing, and the relative health of the participating banks. In practice, however, what emerged was a system manipulated by the banks to enhance their own bottom lines.

The core of the problem was that the rates submitted were based upon "estimates," rather than the actual prices at which banks lent to or borrowed from one another. "There is no reporting of transactions, no one really knows what's going on in the market," said a former senior trader closely involved in setting Libor at a large bank. "You have this vast overhang of financial instruments that hang their own fixes off a rate that doesn't actually exist."[9] Another problem is that those involved in setting the rates had every incentive to lie, since their banks stood to profit or lose money depending on the level at which LIBOR was set each day. Many of the traders involved in the scandal earned millions in profits on derivatives positions which were linked to Libor. Moreover, because the system presumed that the participating banks were truthful in their rate submissions, there was a natural tendency to show the market that you could borrow money at a rate relatively no higher or lower than your competitors. Banks that were weak and having a more difficult time in funding themselves would not have wanted to signal that fact by submitting honest estimates of the high price they would have to pay to borrow. This reality further fueled behavior that sought to conceal the actual financial health of participating banks. This was made manifestly clear during the 2008 financial crisis, when Barclays and other banks purposely submitted rates well below their true borrowing costs.

While there were numerous banks and traders involved in the deception and manipulation of the market, a few have come forward since the scandal and made their views known about what happened, the industry, and the environments in which they operated. One has served jail time, Alex Pabon, a former trader for Barclays in London. Another, perhaps the most recognizable face of the scandal, Tom Hayes, a former Citibank trader, is serving an 11-year sentence in the UK, and then there is Alexis Stenfors, a former Merrill Lynch trader, who has authored a book about the episode.

There are some familiar echoes from the FX rigging scandal that emerge in the commentaries from the three former Libor traders. That perhaps shouldn't come as a surprise given the worlds in which they operated. These were relatively closed environments, populated with similar personalities who were engaged in the type of frenetic activity that can take its toll on both mind and body. They were all feted and courted by banks to work for them given their past money-making track records, and they all eventually came to similar conclusions regarding the ethics and morals of their actions and those they worked with. Some might see their comments as excuses, or self-justifying commentaries to deflect personal blame. Certainly, some of that might be at play. But more importantly, the common themes that emerge should be what interest us, what makes us take notice, and wish to understand better.

According to Alex Pabon, the ex-Barclays trader who has since left the industry after serving time for involvement in the Libor rigging scandal, one needs to look at the larger picture, not just the actions of a few traders. In a 2017 interview, he notes, for example, how a trader who replaced him on the trading desk picked up right where he left off in entering false Libor rates.[10]

"[Y]ou've got to ask why and look at the broader view and go 'ok maybe these guys didn't understand what was wrong,'" said Pabon, adding that while he followed instructions to set LIBOR a certain way, he was not doing so mindlessly. Still, given the hierarchical nature of how the business was structured, and the years of experience behind those in charge, the environment didn't lend itself to challenging common practices. "Your boss is more experienced and you assume there is a reason [behind the order]," said Pabon.

With Tom Hayes, the ex-Citibank trader, we also find that his actions did not occur in a vacuum, devoid of management knowledge. Hayes became widely known in the industry for his masterminding of so-called switch trades, or what are also known as "wash trades." Specifically, in exchange for a broker's help to allegedly distort Libor rates, Hayes would reward brokers by executing fake trades to pay them large commissions. To arrange the "switch trades," Hayes and individual brokers contacted traders at other major banks, including RBS, Merrill Lynch, and JPMorgan, to match trades that Hayes would put through the brokers in order to cancel each other out, earning the brokers commissions in the process. It was compensation for helping to keep Libor rates artificially low. David Enrich's book, *The Spider Network: The Wild Story of a Math Genius, a Gang of Backstabbing Bankers, and One of the Greatest Scams in Financial History*,[11] describes how Hayes would periodically check with his Citibank manager, Mike Pieri, on proposed trades that he knew were suspect. "By paying commissions on meaningless trades, in exchange for receiving help manipulating Libor, Hayes and the brokers were engaging in what most people would regard as fraud for

2 The Financial Crisis: The Culture Problem Emerges

hire," writes Enrich. "To be sure, there were no specific company policies against the practice nor laws that explicitly forbade using switch trades to compensate for Libor manipulation. But even if the word *fraud* didn't cross their minds, the participants should have been under no illusion that the switches were kosher. Hayes justified the deals to himself by the fact that he had received Pieri's permission."

As Enrich describes the early days of the "switch trades" practice with brokers, he writes: "Hayes walked over to Pieri's desk. 'Look, I've done a couple of trades with Terry in and out,' he told his boss. 'I just need to pay him some brokerage. I just wanted to check is that alright.' Pieri said it was fine."

"It wouldn't be hard to construe the behavior as collusive, as a conspiracy to move Libor in ways that had absolutely nothing to do with a bank's estimated borrowing costs," Enrich writes. "The thought had certainly occurred to Hayes at times; for comfort, he told himself that Pieri (his boss) knew exactly what he was doing, which surely would provide him with cover if things ever went wrong."

What we learn from Pabon and Hayes is how easy it was to cross the line of what constituted fraud, and how little guidance was provided when an employee came upon gray areas; where there were no red lines, no explicit boundaries telling you where your limits were.

Alexis Stenfors, who was a star trader for Merrill Lynch during the same period, delves a bit deeper into world of trading and the effect it can have on moral and ethical decision-making.

"Where do you draw the line between the morals of the bank and the morals you hold yourself … Should any such line be drawn at all," asks Stenfors in his memoir, *Barometer of Fear: An Insider's Account of Rogue Trading and the Greatest Banking Scandal in History*.[12] On the face of it the questions are alarming. It suggests abandoning one's own ethics and morals for the greater good of the firm you work for, and accepting whatever the prevailing ethos is at the time. But Stenfors's question also underscores the choices many employees likely face in hyper-competitive trading environments.

In a lengthy *Wall Street Journal* profile in 2016 we get a deeper look into the process whereby Stenfors has attempted to reconcile what he knows was morally wrong within the environment in which he operated.[13] Stenfors joined Merrill Lynch's London office in 2005. At the time, he says his managers encouraged him to take on risky trades and shoot for "nine-digit annual profits." Stenfors's speciality was trading derivatives linked to benchmark rates such as Libor. On the opposite side of many of his trades was Tom Hayes at UBS in Tokyo. Both traders shared a broker, R. P. Martin Holding Ltd.'s Terry Farr. While Hayes was ultimately prosecuted for manipulating Libor, Stenfors was not implicated in the scheme. According to the Journal's profile, Stenfors traded instruments linked to Libor and had noticed what seemed like suspicious movements, which he ultimately concluded was some form of manipulation. He, however, was unaware of Hayes's actions. Using derivatives pegged to currencies and interest rates, Stenfors made a gigantic bet that the financial crisis of 2008 would continue to ravage markets well into 2009, according to the article. Many rivals in the market viewed his position with skepticism. He would either earn millions in profits, or stand to lose everything. When markets stabilized in 2009 Stenfors incurred heavy losses on his positions, and given the magnitude of the trades there was no easy way to unwind them on the market.

Stenfors tried to mask the losses on his books with the hope that the market might turn around and bail him out. If the market did turn his way, his cheating wouldn't have mattered, or at least that was his rationale at the time. The market, however, didn't cooperate, and eventually, senior management uncovered the losses which cost Merrill Lynch $456 million. Stenfors was fired from the firm and banned from the industry for five years. No criminal action was taken.

Looking back on the episode, Stenfors was initially furious with the bank for encouraging him to take on so much risk, and resented the industry for its "no-holds-barred culture." But with the passage of time he became more reflective, acknowledging that during this period he didn't see $100 million as "being a lot of money." Stenfors is now a lecturer on behavioral finance at the UK's University of Portsmouth, and focuses on why benchmarks get manipulated, and how normally honest people sometimes break the rules. "You begin to lie, maybe consciously, maybe subconsciously," he recently told graduate students in a Portsmouth lecture hall, adding that it becomes difficult to understand how the process begins. A rogue trader, he said, "is a risk taker. It's not a crime. It's violating the mores established by the institution that you work for. It's a rebellion against institutional controls that deny individuals opportunities for self-actualization."

In a separate 2017 interview, Stenfors elaborates further on the moral dilemma he sees within large organizations.[14] "I think it's very clear that you should follow your own morals in this sense, and that's what I wish I had done much earlier," he said. "But it's very easy for me to say: 'Follow your own morals and it will be fine.' But it won't be fine. Because if you break the rules and conventions, you'll begin to run into trouble." He then talks about not being invited to drinks parties, and being denied the trading book you desired or getting a smaller bonus.

The rules and conventions Stenfors alludes to are those that guide the group, or the sub-culture within the larger organization. These are norms that sit outside what is dictated by top management or presented to the public, and are used to justify behavior that put the interests of the traders first and the client second. If one wants to succeed in this environment then one must submit to the governing rules, even though they might clash with your own.

Yet, the rationalization of how the trading world itself might legitimately be exempt from the behavioral norms elsewhere in an organization demonstrates the extent to which sub-cultures can pervert ethical norms and behavior. It's a view that perhaps many of Stenfors's colleagues at the time shared. "Early on I learned to accept that the rules of trading did not always apply to the rest of society or vice versa," writes Stenfors in his memoir. "Despite this, conventions within the dealing room felt logical and everybody seemed to accept them. In the absence of outside regulation, the banks simply wrote the rules themselves, which were then accepted by the rest of the market as well. The environment might not have been pleasant, fair or honest all the time – but even so I did not think of trading as immoral."

In his book, Stenfors has a chapter called, '*Why Did You Do It?*' In trying to answer the question, Stenfors sets the scene in advance of his decision to put on massive trades in currency and index-linked derivatives at the height of the financial crisis. Early in 2009, Stenfors told his manager that he would try to make $150 million for the year. In response, Stenfors writes that his manager "burst out laughing. 'I expect much more than that.'" The risks of trying to target a much higher number were considerable given the market environment. "To have any chance of achieving this, I would have to put on the biggest bets I had ever laid down, seen or heard about in the markets in which I traded," writes Stenfors. "It would have to be done in the middle of the worst financial crisis in generations, in an extremely illiquid and volatile market." In other words, the odds were stacked against him successfully achieving what his manager wanted. He knew this, but went ahead anyway. Here, one might say, is a classic case of an individual behaving irrationally; facing a set of choices of where his potential losses far exceed his possible gains. How does Stenfors reconcile his decision?

"Something inside me must have screamed that it was an impossible task. The bank was underestimating how difficult markets were. They were also overestimating my ability to perform miracles. But I avoided such thoughts," says Stenfors. "I convinced myself that it was the right thing to do, and in doing so made a spectacular error of judgment." Once he discovers the size of his losses, Stenfors tells us that he should have alerted his manager to the situation, but says, "I did not trust him." He doesn't explain why there was a lack of trust between the two, but one can imagine from their prior exchange that his manager perhaps had enormous pressure placed upon him to deliver spectacular results. The importance of the "middle man," the manager who sits between the employee and upper management plays a critical role in upholding the values and ethics of an organization, but will no doubt encounter business objectives that conflict and put those values at risk. It's clear, not only in Stenfors's case, but also for Hayes and Pabon, that expectations and guidance by their managers factored into their decision-making process, rightly or wrongly. With Stenfors, we never quite get to a satisfactory answer about his motivations to cover up his massive losses, and are left with more questions about his character and what seems to be a misplaced sense of loyalty and judgment. "I should have resigned. But the loyalty I felt – however misguided – was too strong," he says. "After years of discussing morality with a lawyer, two years with a psychotherapist, and several more years talking about it with people I have met since, I am not sure whether I have come any closer to a definitive answer to the question: 'Why did you do it?' Perhaps getting the answer was less important than *seeking* an answer."

Perhaps one of the more important takeaways from what Stenfors has described in understanding his actions is why someone else in similar circumstances might have made different choices.

Goldman's 'Abacus': The Customer Comes Second

Goldman Sachs's storied history on Wall Street owes to many things, but over the course of the firm's 149-year existence what has stood it apart from others was its focus on clients, and perhaps no other executive embodied the culture of putting client interests first than Sidney Weinberg, who ran the company from 1930 to 1969. The elfish character—he stood only five feet four inches tall—worked his way up the company ladder, starting as a porter's assistant. Weinberg's guiding principle was that if the firm won the trust of its clients it would prosper.[15] Weinberg avoided risky bets, and the understated culture he instilled in the firm served it well for many decades. According to George Doty, a partner during Weinberg's reign, "Sidney Weinberg's fondest word was *integrity*. He virtually worshipped that word, and what it meant for him – honesty and putting customers' interests first."[16]

During the late 1980s and early 1990s, however, the direction of the firm began to change. Some of the shift was its own choice, others were factors related to competitive industry demands as well as regulatory change. Under the stewardship of Stephen Friedman and Robert Rubin, who both shared the senior partner position from 1990 until 1992—Rubin then left to work for the Clinton administration and became Treasury Secretary in 1995—Goldman began to embrace more risk. The firm expanded the trading side of the business, particularly in fixed-income securities. Goldman had long established itself as trusted advisers to major corporations, and earned much of its money from arranging public offerings and mergers, the bread and butter of investment banking. Trading was a new venture, but one the firm believed it needed to undertake given intense competition from other Wall Street houses. As Lisa Endlich writes in *Goldman Sachs— The Culture of Success*, Goldman ranked fifth in total bond underwritings in 1984, behind Salomon Brothers, Drexel Lambert, First Boston, and Merrill Lynch.[17] "Salomon had a 26 percent share of the underwriting market while Goldman Sachs had just 10 percent. But the fixed-income business was becoming integral to every other part of investment banking; unless the department could be brought up to the standards of the rest of the businesses, the entire firm would suffer."

Yet during this period of transformational change, Goldman was still a partnership. It embodied many of the same cultural principles laid down by Weinberg senior, and later his son, John L. Weinberg and John Whitehead, both of whom maintained the focus on client interest. One of the biggest tests of the firm's cultural cohesion came with the arrest of Robert Freeman in 1987, as noted earlier. Freeman was a partner and head of the firm's risk arbitrage unit, a very profitable business for Goldman for many years, and from which Robert Rubin made his reputation. During the 1980s the risk arbitrage business on Wall Street had grown enormously, led by mercurial figures such as Ivan Boesky, a risk arbitrageur who was immensely successful, although some had doubts about his business practices. On November 14, 1986, Boesky was arrested for insider trading, pled guilty to the charges and paid a fine of $100 million, a sum that was unprecedented at the time. But Boesky did not go quietly. As part of his deal with U.S. authorities, he implicated Martin Siegel, a well-respected merger expert who had recently moved from Kidder Peabody to Drexel Burnham Lambert. Siegel apparently collaborated with Boesky, accepting suitcases of cash in exchange for information about upcoming takeovers. Boesky, it seemed, was not quite as clever as many thought, having had a direct pipeline of information flowing from Siegel and others with insider knowledge of corporate decisions.

Siegel, in turn, pointed the finger at Freeman of Goldman. The allegations against Freeman prompted the firm to get ahead of U.S. law enforcement agencies, and led to a sweeping internal investigation of Freeman's business unit, which included an exhaustive examination of its trading records and scores of interviews with members of the arbitrage desk. Nothing suspicious or unusual was uncovered. As Goldman's top lawyer, Lawrence Pedowitz, explained: "These were transactions that any firm that was in the arbitrage flow would have been trading in substantial volume. Virtually all of the trades were explainable in light of public record information. The transactions did not look irregular."[18] The internal investigation included reconstructing conversations that were not recorded—a practice now almost ubiquitous among Wall Street firms. Many of Goldman's businesses routinely taped conversations with clients as a "final check in any dispute with a counterparty." The publicity that ensued from Siegel's allegations was not favorable. Certain clients began to question whether dealing with Goldman was wise. As Endlich writes, a certain partner of the firm's equities business complained to senior management that a "counterpart had begun to use tape recorders, and the partner was thinking of discontinuing the relationship. Investment banking was a gentlemen's business, he felt; trust was the cornerstone, and he was not certain his division wanted to deal with people who did not hold the same values." The partner was reluctantly informed that on the trading side of the house taping phone conversations with clients was a normal course of business. (The observation and distinction between the two different businesses and the practices used with clients bear highlighting, as this has become part of a more fundamental structural shift in business on Wall Street.)

As Goldman's internal investigation into Freeman's business dealings proved fruitless, the firm's partners were relatively confident that the widening scandal of insider trading would not implicate the company. That is, until the morning of February 12, 1987. Special Deputy U.S. Marshall Thomas Doonan and two postal inspectors came onto the twenty-ninth-floor trading room at Goldman, found Freedman, and asked him to step inside his glass-fronted office. They told him he was under arrest. Freedman claimed innocence and the firm backed him. Goldman fought hard and long for Freedman's innocence. The stakes were enormous. Given the partnership structure, the firm's partners were personally financially liable for any potential fines. More important, however, was the risk of reputational damage should a criminal conviction occur. As Endlich notes, there are two ways of looking at the dilemma the firm faced: "Most within the firm think that Freedman was defended so vigorously because his partners believe in his

2 The Financial Crisis: The Culture Problem Emerges

innocence. This may be true, but Goldman Sachs would have had to fight – and win – the battle in any case."

On April 9, 1987, Freeman was indicted on federal charges of conspiracy to violate securities laws. Freeman remained a partner with the firm during the trial and Goldman paid for his hefty legal expenses. "No one within Goldman Sachs broke ranks, a reflection in part of an institutional culture that had placed the firm ahead of its institutional partners for generations," wrote journalist James Stewart in his book on insider trading scandals.[19]

The government's case against Freeman and Siegel suffered a serious of setbacks, as there seemed to be insufficient evidence against the two to prove conspiracy. However, a *Wall Street Journal* article on February 12, 1988[20] that detailed Freeman's involvement with Siegel during the 1985 leveraged buyout of Beatrice Corporation by Kohlberg, Kravis, Roberts and Company (KKR), included an exchange between the two bankers that led Freeman sell a large share of his holdings in Beatrice ahead of a major restructuring of the KKR buyout. The restructuring of the deal led to a sharp decline in the company's stock price, but given Freeman's insider knowledge he had saved the firm $548,000. At this point, Freeman decided to plead guilty to one count of insider trading rather than drag himself and Goldman through a lengthy trial. "The admission of guilt shocked the firm, which had staunchly defended Freeman's innocence, and spent tens of millions of dollars on his defense," writes Endlich. Freeman defended his guilty plea as a way to put the matter behind him and the firm. After Freeman's admission of guilt, the government dropped a further investigation of Goldman. In a letter to its staff, Goldman's management committee wrote: "We do not condone even a single act of wrongdoing. However, it remains true that over the past thirty months, Bob had been subjected to an arrest that the prosecutor has since characterized as a mistake, a withdrawn indictment, and a series of highly publicized formal allegations and innuendos that far exceed anything he actually did... He and his family have our heartfelt sympathy." The episode, one of the most difficult for Goldman, Freeman and his family, demonstrated that the "culture of the partnership ran deep. Even as Freeman served time, his partners would not abandon him," Endlich noted.

It is hard to imagine any Wall Street firm today launching the type of defense of an employee that Goldman did with Robert Freeman. But Goldman was a partnership at the time, not the corporate entity it is today. As we will see, the internal culture of a partnership differs greatly with that of a corporation, particularly when it comes to management oversight and accountability when things go wrong. The economic forces in the industry that ultimately forced Goldman toward a corporate structure dovetailed with the changed nature of its business model. In many ways, the strategic business shift Goldman undertook during the 1980s were the seeds of what some have called "transactional" banking; a departure from the more traditional forms of relationship banking, where bankers would spend countless hours with their clients to understand their businesses and financial needs. Goldman was not alone in raising the profile of its fixed-income trading operations. Other banks also expanded their footprint in capital market activities, which soon became a major source of revenue, overtaking traditional lending or other corporate banking businesses. Yet, trading is, by its very nature, a much more impersonal business. While there is a client on the other end of the phone, the relationship is not quite as intimate as when you are seeking to help the same client raise funds for a major expansion of its manufacturing plant, for example. From the 1980s onward, transactional banking has become the prime engine of profitability for many Wall Street and foreign banks. The revenue contribution from so-called "FICC" businesses—fixed-income, currencies and commodities—grew sharply after 1999 when two provisions of the Glass–Steagall Act—the 1930s legislative reform that separated commercial from investment banking—were repealed; specifically, those that restricted affiliations between banks and securities firms. For Goldman Sachs, trading had become its dominant money maker. By 1999, revenue generated from what was called trading and principal investments was 43% of net revenues. Investment banking, which included underwriting and financial advisory, represented 33% of net revenues.[21]

There were other signs of a departure from old work habits. Goldman also began to shift its traditional role within its mergers and acquisition business during the 1990s. For many decades, the firm would never support hostile takeover bidders, or raiders. Goldman had made a strategic decision not to represent companies initiating hostile bids, the only large investment banking firm to do so. As a result, CEOs were more comfortable revealing confidential information to Goldman than to other firms, because they trusted Goldman not to use the information in representing hostile raiders against them, according to Steven Mandis, a former Goldman executive, and now adjunct professor at Columbia University's business school.[22] "This policy lost Goldman some business and restricted the profits and growth of the M&A department, but it was a sound business decision that contributed to the positive public perception of the company. It was long-term greedy, calculated to make the most money for the firm over the long term, and

2 The Financial Crisis: The Culture Problem Emerges 25

Goldman may well have ultimately made more money because of it," writes Mandis. However, in the late 1990s, this policy was challenged. Many huge hostile deals were announced by Goldman clients and potential clients. One argument used by partners who thought the firm should support hostile raiders was: "If we don't, someone else will." As the hostile takeover business grew on Wall Street, the lost fees associated with not supporting such business became apparent, and while some partners were still reluctant to jump on board, the firm shifted its longstanding policy. "To many of the Goldman partners ... in hindsight, there could hardly have been a more dramatic business policy decision to signal that the Goldman culture was changing," Mandis writes.

The cultural shift, which put the trading side of the house in the driver's seat, and became the primary revenue generator during much of the period from 2000 to 2009, came under increased scrutiny in the more recent past, as other banks, many of them Goldman's direct competitors, chose to diversify their business model and rely less on trading as a major revenue earner. Goldman has followed suit, gradually establishing new businesses such as consumer lending.[23]

The foregoing expose of Goldman's history, how it evolved from its partnership model, and all that represented, to its current public structure, is not without purpose. The changes to the firm's internal culture along this transformational path may have contributed to the scandal in collateralized debt obligations during the 2008 financial crisis, and highlighted how far the firm had deviated from the principles of its former leaders.

Had he been alive, it is hard to judge what Sidney Weinberg would have made of the "ABACUS" scandal that engulfed Goldman Sachs in 2010. It might have pushed him over the proverbial edge, or he might have simply viewed it as the natural outcome of a long progression of changes at the firm—and more broadly the industry, if not society—that placed less of a premium on ethics or integrity. Indeed, he might have concluded that he was happy to have worked in finance when he did, a period when the relationship between employee, manager and customer was in many ways seamless; each working toward a common goal or shared purpose that would benefit all. It was a period when relationships mattered, and if there is anything that demonstrated how far Goldman had fallen from that ethos, "ABACUS 2007-AC1," as it appeared on the SEC's complaint in April 2010, represented the absolute bottom.[24]

The backdrop to the case concerns the U.S. housing market in the period leading up to 2007 and the financial crisis that ensued. Goldman, along with many firms on Wall Street, took part in structuring complex derivatives products that had as its underlying asset residential mortgages of varying quality. These so-called synthetic collateralized debt obligations, or CDOs, were tied to the performance of subprime residential mortgage-backed securities ("RMBS") and were structured and marketed by Goldman in early 2007 when the housing market and related securities were beginning to show signs of distress. For investors, the attractiveness of such products was the relatively high yield when compared with other investments. One such product, ABACUS 2007-AC1, contained residential mortgage securities of varying degrees of quality. Some were a better credit risk than others, and a third party, or outside firm, ACA Management LLC ("ACA"), was assigned with selecting the securities that comprised ABACUS. The company, as stated in Goldman's marketing material, had experience in analyzing credit risk in RMBS. However, what Goldman didn't disclose in its marketing prose was that ACA was not the only third party involved in selecting which securities would go into the product. One of Goldman's top clients, John Paulson, who ran his own hedge fund, Paulson & Co., also had a hand in the selection process. Specifically, as the SEC documented, Goldman "arranged a transaction at Paulson's request in which Paulson heavily influenced the selection of the portfolio to suit its economic interests, but failed to disclose to investors, as part of the description of the portfolio selection process contained in the marketing materials used to promote the transaction, Paulson's role in the portfolio selection process or its adverse economic interests." Paulson selected securities that he knew were about to "experience credit events" in the near future—in order words, they were bound to fail. He, in turn, took a short position against the ABACUS product, confident that as the market for the RMBS contained in the product would deteriorate, he would stand to profit. None of this was disclosed to the outside investors to whom Goldman marketed the product.

At the center of the case was Fabrice Tourre, a French-born Goldman vice president. Tourre was primarily responsible for the ABACUS product. According to the SEC complaint, he "devised the transaction, prepared the marketing materials and communicated directly with investors." Tourre also knew of Paulson's undisclosed short interest and the hedge fund's role in the collateral selection process. In addition, Tourre misled ACA into believing that Paulson invested approximately $200 million in the equity of ABACUS (a long position), and that Paulson's interests in the process were aligned with ACA's. Paulson's interests were, in fact, sharply conflicting. When the deal closed in April 2007, Paulson paid Goldman approximately $15 million for structuring and marketing the product. By October of the same year, 83% of the RMBS in ABACUS had been downgraded by rating agencies. By early 2008, 99% of the portfolio had been downgraded. Those who invested in ABACUS, which included a large German bank, lost over $1 billion. Meanwhile, Paulson's short position in the product yield approximately a $1 billion profit.[25]

Goldman settled the case against the SEC for $550 million, the largest fine ever paid by a Wall Street firm up to that time. The firm also admitted that the ABACUS marketing material "contained incomplete information." Tourre, however, sought to fight for his innocence. As Eugene Soltes[26] writes in *Why They Do It: Inside the Mind of the White-Collar Criminal*: "Nothing struck Tourre as intuitively wrong with the transaction he helped design. He believed it complied with the law. In fact, waiting in his attorney's office for the verdict, Tourre reflected on the charges against him. 'If there was something wrong with this transaction,' Tourre asked, 'wouldn't people have told me?'" The unanimous guilty verdict baffled Tourre. "If the ABACUS transaction was so overtly fraudulent, why didn't any of his superiors or colleagues at Goldman Sachs tell him," Soltes adds. Indeed, some critics of the case later wrote of how the SEC failed to go after Tourre's managers, who must have had knowledge of the conflicts and deception that was involved. In a 2016 article for *The New Yorker*,[27] Jesse Eisinger detailed the internal struggles at the SEC during the ABACUS investigation, and how senior agency officials were reluctant to go after senior Goldman executives. The reason they gave was a lack of evidence, but others argued the "driving force was something subtler." In the view of one SEC official who was part of the case, the agency was "captured" by Wall Street, "a psychological process in which officials become increasingly gun shy in the face of criticism from their bosses, Congress, and the industry the agency is supposed to oversee."

There are additional aspects of the case that show how misaligned Goldman's interests were with its clients: the firm itself took short positions in ABACUS to profit from its decline. But perhaps one of the more telling developments that further exposed the firm's thinking and culture came in a separate class action lawsuit from a company shareholder, Ilene Richman.[28] Richman sued Goldman, and four of its senior executives, accusing them of defrauding investors in the ABACUS deal. In the suit, Richman described the frequent public statements made by the firm's executives explaining how important integrity was to Goldman. For example, according to Goldman's statement of its own "Business Principles and Standards," they said: "[We] are dedicated to complying fully with the letter and spirit of the laws, rules, and ethical principles that govern us. Our continued success depends upon unswerving adherences to this standard." In Richman's view the ABACUS transaction violated these principles, and the firm defrauded its own shareholders by not abiding by the firm's own statements regarding integrity and not following the "letter and spirit" of the law. In the suit, Richman demonstrated the impact the ABACUS had on Goldman's share price, leading to sizeable declines and loss in shareholder value.

What was Goldman's response to Richman's allegations? Attorneys for Goldman, who sought to have the suit dismissed said, "[T]he vast majority of the supposed 'misstatements' alleged in the compliant – e.g., regarding the firm's 'integrity' and 'honesty' – are nothing more than classic 'puffery' or statements of opinion." To sum up, the firm's statements about ethics and integrity didn't mean much, and are nothing more than standard marketing material. No one should take these words at face value. The judge presiding over the case, U.S. District Court Judge Paul Crotty, replied:

> Goldman's arguments in this respect are Orwellian. Words such as "honesty," "integrity," and "fair dealing" apparently do not mean what they say; they do not set standards; they are mere shibboleths. If Goldman's claim of "honesty" and "integrity" are simply puffery, the world of finance may be in more trouble than we recognize.

The class action suit has remained mired in court proceedings since 2011, with Goldman seeking dismissal of the case. In August 2018, Judge Crotty said the investors may again pursue class action claims that the bank concealed conflicts of interest when creating the ABACUS product. His decision reversed an earlier appeals court ruling saying the burden of proof on Goldman was set too high for the firm to effectively rebut the case.[29]

Wells Fargo: Breakdown in Governance

In December 2014, Thomson Reuters published an interview with Patricia Callahan, who at the time was Chief Administrative Officer for Wells Fargo, responsible for corporate communication and government relations.[30] A 36-year veteran of the company, Callahan had served as head of Compliance and Enterprise Risk Management, providing regulatory compliance oversight for the company. She spoke about banking culture, and what it meant for Wells Fargo, among other issues. The bank had long heralded its internal culture, often pointing to its "Visions and Values" document, which outlined the company's values. When asked how Wells Fargo instilled its culture in practice, Callahan said: "We've been at this for a long time and the messages have been consistent. If there is one thing that I know about culture is that if you want people to know what to expect of them you have say it a lot, and it has to be consistent, and it has to be believed and understood at all levels in the company. It's not the kind of thing that the CEO does alone." Callahan noted that because the bank had worked on cultural issues for many years it had learned new ways of getting the message across to its employees. "*But the main message is that we're in business for our customers. Our customers need to be successful if we're going to be successful. And that message is the one that's out there in front — that this is a business about customers*," said Callahan. When asked about the view among some U.S. regulators that large financial institutions have increasingly looked at their customers as "counterparties," rather than clients, and that under such circumstances, customers can be seen more as a transactional opportunity, Callahan replied: "[T]hat is really not true at Wells Fargo. Part of that is a different business model. We do a lot of business with consumers where clearly they are customers … The way we operate and our business model require that all of our businesses are successful with our customers."

Callahan retired from Wells Fargo not too long after the interview, and before the bank became engulfed in the so-called "phantom" account scandal from which it is still working to restore the reputational damage suffered. The account scandal, unveiled by Federal regulators in 2016, charged that employees of the bank secretly created millions of unauthorized bank and credit card accounts without their customers knowing it. The factors behind opening such accounts appeared to have come from intense management pressure on employees to meet certain financial targets. Wells Fargo's financial success over the years owed much to its "cross-selling" business model, whereby existing customers are encouraged to take on new products and services. The model is not unique, but Wells Fargo appeared to have mastered the ability to expand its relationship with existing customers, more than most banks. What emerged from the investigation of the account scandal was a "soul-crushing" culture of fear and intimidation by managers, where employees were pressured to reach extreme, and often unrealistic, sales goals. Some broke the law by opening new accounts without the customer's knowledge. In reaction to the scandal, the bank fired 5300 employees. The head of the retail sales unit where the fake accounts were manufactured, Carrie Tolstedt, took early retirement and was allowed to collect a bonus of $124 million. The bank's chief executive, John Stumpf, after mounting an unconvincing defense of the bank's culture before a U.S. Congressional committee, stepped down in October 2016.[31] Evidence continued to mount of a severe breakdown in corporate governance and oversight. In early 2017, Wells Fargo acknowledged there were signs it had retaliated against workers who tried to blow the whistle on the fake accounts. News accounts emerged of employees being terminated after using the company's hotline to unveil information about customer fraud.[32]

Also in 2017, new allegations emerged that the bank modified existing customer mortgages without authorization from the clients. The allegations said such changes resulted in customers paying the bank more than they owed. Additional weaknesses have been uncovered in other parts of the organization, such as wealth management. Reflecting the growing frustration among U.S. regulators with the slow pace of management reform, and actions to instill more effective controls over its various businesses, the Federal Reserve in February 2018 took the unprecedented step to bar Wells Fargo from increasing its total asset size until the bank had improved its governance and controls.[33] In addition, four directors of the bank were forced to leave, a direct consequence of the Fed's regulatory action. Whether the focus of regulators on the directors and governance process at Wells Fargo is a signal of things to come for the broader industry may be difficult to judge. However, many critics of the industry claim that senior executives and directors have not been held sufficiently accountable for the misdeeds of their organizations, with the costs too often falling upon lower-level employees, as well as shareholders, who in the end bear the burden of regulatory fines. In each of the prior three scandals examined—FX, Libor and ABACUS at Goldman Sachs—there are questions over how much senior managers knew of what their front-line employees were engaged in. One wonders whether there was clearly no knowledge of fraudulent behavior or a selective case of willful blindness. As we shall see, one of major problems of instilling strong ethical and cultural values at large and complex organizations is simply their size—they might simply be too big to manage. In the case of Wells Fargo, there clearly seemed to be either a void of information filtering to the upper ranks of the organization, or if the information was conveyed it was either not believed or ignored.

Ousted CEO John Stumpf gave, what was for many, a stupefying performance when appearing before Congress. According to Stumpf's testimony, a board committee became aware of consumer fraud "at a high level" in 2011. There was then a broader investigation and discussion around 2013 and 2014, prompted in part by media reports of alleged fraudulent behavior. Stumpf testified that he personally became aware of the fraud in 2013, when after two years of trying to curb the problem, the volume of fake accounts was still rising. However, it then took another two years before Stumpf hired external consultants in 2015 to determine the scope of the problem and the damage inflicted on the bank's customers.

The "transactional" nature of the bank's relationship with its customers was vividly highlighted when Stumpf noted that the bank didn't realize customers could be charged fees for these fake accounts. However, later, "when we finally connected the dots on customer harm in 2015, the board was very active on this," said Stumpf. As Susan M. Ochs, a financial services expert at think tank New America, wrote at the time: "This statement implies that the only impact on consumers is monetary: wrongful fees. When the bank thought thousands of employees were simply violating consumer trust — stealing identities, forging signatures, secretly moving money — that wasn't enough harm to provoke the board's active involvement." This misjudgment, says Ochs, might explain why the bank's board dragged its feet and only imposed penalties on its executives until after the first Congressional hearing.[34]

Before leaving the bank, Stumpf refused to be drawn into a debate on the company's culture. In his view, the problems uncovered were operational or compliance-related, highlighting just how far removed both he and his management team were from the business practices of the organization. An independent directors report highlighted many of these failures, including the bank's risk committee's failure to ask for basic information, with the most glaring omission being the lack of knowledge about the dismissal of 5000 employees until Wells Fargo settled its initial enforcement action with U.S. agencies.[35] But there was more—much more. The human resources function at Wells Fargo was decentralized, meaning each business unit had its own HR group, an arrangement that made curbing sales practices that were perceived as detrimental to the firm more difficult, particularly if the business unit was run by individuals very powerful, and unwilling to act upon HR concerns. The directors' report found this to be the case with the "Community Bank" run by Tolstedt. "While recognizing many of the serious issues posed by sales pressure and improper sales practices, the HR function in the Community Bank was either unable or unwilling to effectively challenge Community Bank leadership on the sales model that resulted in the sales practice issues, and did not effectively escalate the issues outside the Community Bank," the report said. A decentralized approach was also used in developing compensation plans at the bank, further removing effective oversight. "While all incentive compensation plans were required to comply with the Wells Fargo's Incentive Compensation Risk Management ("ICRM") policy adopted in 2011, the design and review of the Community Bank's incentive compensation plans was the primary responsibility of the Community Bank, with limited involvement by Corporate HR and Corporate Risk," the directors' report noted. "Nonetheless, Corporate HR was the 'owner' of the ICRM program, and the HR Director was the chair of the Incentive Compensation Steering Committee (composed of members of the ERMC), which retained authority over all incentive compensation plans." Senior executives at the firm, including Callahan, were aware of the disturbing number of employee firings at the Community Bank, and the incentive and compensation plans that led to such dismissals. The report notes that as chief administrative officer, Callahan "had been aware of sales practice issues in the Community Bank going back to 2002, when she was involved in dealing with the misconduct at the branch in Colorado." However, it wasn't until late 2013, and after a Los Angeles Times investigative article was published about the Community Bank's practices, that Callahan and another top executive "asked a senior Corporate HR person and a senior employment lawyer to work with the Community Bank in analyzing the causes of the sales practice issue and recommending measures to address those causes." However, even this high-level effort did not appear to have had a significant impact on the actions taken by the Community Bank in late 2013 to early 2014, the report concluded.

When viewing the Goldman and Wells Fargo cases side-by-side, it might at first seem difficult to find similar patterns. But a bit of historical perspective, and the evolution of banking over the past decades, can suggest a few parallels. First, the history. Both firms have a long, vaunted history in U.S. financial services. We've already examined the Goldman story at a high level, with the firm established in 1869. For Wells Fargo, its beginnings were formed in 1852 in the western part of America, after Henry Wells and William G. Fargo created the American Express Company in New York in 1850. When American Express declined to extend their business to California, Wells and Fargo founded a new banking and express company in 1852 to serve the western frontier—Wells, Fargo and Company.

The focus on the customer was always paramount, and the brand, embellished with stage coaches, is one that has lasted through generations and numerous financial upheavals in the United States. However, things started to change when the bank merged with Norwest in 1998. That's when the combined entity put "cross-selling" at the heart of its business model. Wells Fargo refers to its branches as "stores," and they announce their cross-sell ratio during quarterly conference calls. They have often stated that their goal is to sell every customer at least eight of its financial products—checking and savings accounts, mortgages, car loans, and so on. But with sales targets come incentives, and as we saw in Goldman's case, incentives can sometimes become misaligned against the customer.

Commenting on customer scandal, Warren Buffett told Berkshire Hathaway investors in early 2017 that Wells Fargo "incentivized the wrong type of behavior." Buffet's company is the largest shareholder in Wells Fargo. In Buffett's view, the largest mistake made by management was not acting quickly enough once they found out they had a problem. "If there's a major problem, the CEO will get wind of it. At that moment, that's the key to everything. The CEO has to act," Buffett said. "The main problem was they didn't act when they learned about it."[36]

What exacerbated an already bad situation was the company's treatment of its employees. After the sales scandal came to light, there were numerous media articles highlighting how whistleblowers inside the bank had been telling executives of the problem for years. But instead of listening to these employees, and following up on their information, Wells Fargo retaliated against them. In some cases, whistleblowers were fired in such a way that they had no hope of finding another job in financial services.

Goldman's business model shift came gradually as the trading side of the firm gained in importance and its contribution to the bottom line increased. Once the firm went public, those "transactional" businesses expanded, and along with the growth of trading the leadership of the firm changed to reflect the importance of these businesses. At Wells Fargo, a cross-selling model, that is increasingly reliant on technology to interact with customers, puts ever greater distance between the bank and customer. The latter becomes a "counterparty" to whom one can sell a growing number of products and services. As the distance grows between the bank and the customer, it becomes more difficult to put an actual face behind the name. As such, it is harder to gauge the harm you might be doing a customer if that individual is removed and increasingly anonymous. This is also the case with a business model that emphasizes trading and the execution of transactions with customers—they become removed, less visible to those supposedly serving their interests. In both cases, money becomes the determining factor in the relationship; how to extract the most for the benefit of the organization rather than protecting the interests of the clients and maintaining the fiduciary responsibility entrusted to you. In both scandals, fiduciary duty went by the wayside in favor of maximizing profitability.

There is little reason to doubt that Patricia Callahan was forthright and believed in the core principles of Wells Fargo's culture and ethics when interviewed in 2014, even as the behavior that was later uncovered was occurring at the time. Whether the very top of Goldman's management hierarchy was aware of the intricacies of the ABACUS deal is open to question. We will likely never know the answer. Sometimes there is knowledge at the very top of an organization that your lieutenants are engaged in misconduct and wrongdoing—witness the Enron scandal. But more often the intelligence at the top is less than complete. Information tends to move upward more slowly, particularly if it's bad news. Turned around, the message from on high gets filtered down through the ranks in an uneven fashion, and by the time it reaches the middle-tier of large firms, it might seem little more than corporate speak. What matters for those on the front lines who are charged with meeting their sales or revenue targets is doing what they can within the gray areas of legality, and hopefully not cross the line. Both Goldman Sachs and Wells Fargo are large, complex organizations, each containing numerous businesses and cultural silos that may often run to their own tune. Organizational size is something that many of the leaders of such firms cherish and applaud; scale is a positive factor, allowing them to better service their customer needs, many of whom have a global footprint. While this may be true, establishing and maintaining a coherent and uniform culture can become more challenging. All of the management information systems you have at your disposal may be uniformly signaling "green," that all is going according to plan. Yet, as we've seen, blind spots can emerge with the potential to inflict serious damage, both financial and reputational.

Notes

1. "Triennial Central Bank Survey of Foreign Exchange and OTC Derivatives Markets in 2016," Bank for International Settlements, updated December 11, 2016.
2. United States District Court Southern District of New York; In Re Foreign Exchange Benchmark Rates Antitrust Litigation; Case Number: 1:13-cv-07789-LGS, filed 7/31/15.
3. "Secret Currency Traders' Club Devised Biggest Market's Rates," Liam Vaughan, Gavin Finch, and Bob Ivry, Bloomberg, December 19, 2013.

4. *Nudge: Improving Decisions About Health, Wealth, and Happiness*, Richard H. Thaler and Cass R. Sunstein, Penguin Books, 2012.
5. New York State Department of Financial Services; In the Matter of Barclays Bank PLC, New York Branch, CONSENT ORDER UNDER NEW YORK BANKING LAW §§ 44 and 44-a; May 20, 2015.
6. London Employment Tribunals; Claimant: Mr. P Stimpson; Case Number: 3200437/15; September 8–11, 15, and 17, 2015.
7. London Employment Tribunals; Claimant: Ms. C. McWilliams; Case Number: 3200384/15; January 25–28, 2016, February 1–2 and 3, 2016.
8. Alternative Reference Rates Committee, Federal Reserve Bank of New York, www.newyorkfed.org/arrc.
9. "The Rotten Heart of Finance," *The Economist*, July 7, 2012.
10. "A Barclays Exec Who Went to Prison for LIBOR-rigging Breaks His Silence," Lianna Brinded, *Business Insider*, April 12, 2017.
11. *The Spider Network: The Wild Story of a Math Genius, a Gang of Backstabbing Bankers, and One of the Greatest Scams in Financial History*, David Enrich, HarperCollins, 2017.
12. *Barometer of Fear: An Insider's Account of Rogue Trading and the Greatest Banking Scandal in History*, Alexis Stenfors, Zed Books Ltd., 2017.
13. "A Disgraced Trader's Struggle for Redemption," David Enrich, *The Wall Street Journal*, April 29, 2016.
14. "What's It Like to Lose £350m? A Rogue Trader Confesses," Andrew Anthony, *The Guardian*, May 7, 2017.
15. "The Firm," John Cassidy, *The New Yorker*, March 8, 1999.
16. *The Partnership: The Making of Goldman Sachs*, Charles D. Ellis, Penguin Press, 2008.
17. *Goldman Sachs—The Culture of Success*, Lisa Endlich, Touchstone, 1999.
18. Ibid., Endlich.
19. *Den of Thieves*, James B. Stewart, Simon & Schuster, 1991.
20. Ibid., Ellis.
21. Data can be found in Goldman Sachs Group 10K; filed with Securities and Exchange Commission; fiscal year ending November 26, 1999, www.goldmansachs.com/investor-relations/financials/archived/10k/docs/1999-10-k.pdf.
22. *What Happened to Goldman Sachs: An Insider's Story of Organizational Drift and Its Unintended Consequences*, Steven Mandis, Harvard Business School Publishing, 2013.
23. "Goldman Targets Credit-card Borrowers with New Lending Business," Olivia Oran, *Reuters*, October 13, 2016.
24. See www.sec.gov/litigation/complaints/2010/comp21489.pdf.
25. "FACTBOX: How Goldman's ABACUS Deal Worked," *Reuters*, April 16, 2010.
26. *Why They Do It: Inside the Mind of the White-Collar Criminal*, Eugene Soltes, Public Affairs, an imprint of Perseus Books LLC, a subsidiary of Hachette Book Group, Inc., 2016.

27. "Why the SEC Didn't Hit Goldman Sachs Harder," Jesse Eisinger, *The New Yorker*, April 21, 2016.
28. U.S. District Court Southern District of New York, March 25, 2011; Case 1:10-cv-03461-PAC: www.law.du.edu/documents/corporate-governance/securities-matters/richman-v-goldman-sachs-group-062512crotty.pdf.
29. "Goldman Shareholders Can Again Pursue Class Action Over CDOs," Jonathan Stempel, *Reuters*, August 14, 2018.
30. "INTERVIEW: U.S. Fed's Culture Focus Will Take More Dialogue with Banks—Wells Fargo's Callahan," Henry Engler, *Reuters*, December 4, 2014.
31. "Wells Fargo CEO John Stumpf Resigns Amid Scandal," Richard Gonzales, National Public Radio, October 12, 2016.
32. "Wells Fargo Admits to Signs of Worker Retaliation," Matt Egan, CNN Money, January 24, 2017.
33. "Federal Reserve Restricts Wells Fargo's Growth Until Firm Improves Governance and Controls," Board of Governors, Federal Reserve System, Docket No. 18-007-B-HC, February 2, 2018.
34. "The Leadership Blind Spots at Wells Fargo," Susan M. Ochs, *Harvard Business Review*, October 6, 2016.
35. Independent Directors of the Board of Wells Fargo & Company Sales Practices Investigation Report, April 10, 2017: https://www08.wellsfargomedia.com/assets/pdf/about/investor-relations/presentations/2017/board-report.pdf.
36. "Warren Buffett Slams Wells Fargo's Handling of Massive Sales Scandal," Kristine Phillips, *The Washington Post*, May 7, 2017.

3

Culture and Organizational Size

The following Table 3.1 lists the most active players in the global foreign exchange market and their respective share of the marketplace in 2018 and 2017.

As can be seen from the figures, the top five institutions—which includes one electronic trading platform—controlled 40% of the market in 2018.[1] In the 2015 U.S. District Court complaint against the 13 banks alleged to have fixed the benchmark prices of currencies in the market, it was estimated that the group had a combined market share of over 90%. If you add up the market share percentages for the ten organizations listed above for 2018, the total is 65%. If we added in three more banks, their market share would be 75%—not the 90% mark seen in 2015, but still dominant. The size and influence of these banks is not limited to the foreign exchange market, however. If one looks at other markets, similar patterns emerge. For example, data on the primary dealer market for U.S. Treasury securities, of which there are currently 23 banks and firms who are designated by the Federal Reserve Bank of New York to make markets in Treasuries, shows that the top five dealers have a market share across most maturities of close to 50%.[2] Many of these institutions are the same ones found dominant in the foreign exchange market. Indeed, there is currently a class action lawsuit in U.S. Federal courts alleging that several of the top banks in the Treasury market colluded to manipulate prices in the auctions for securities from 2007 to 2015. The plaintiffs in the case, many of them institutional investors, argue the banks sold them Treasury securities at above market prices after colluding with one another.[3] The methods by which the dealers communicated

Table 3.1 FX liquidity providers

Rank 2018	Rank 2017	Liquidity provider	Market share 2018* (%)	2017 (%)
1	2	JPMorgan	12.13	10.34
2	3	UBS	8.25	7.56
3	12	XTX markets	7.36	3.29
4	4	Bank of America Merrill Lynch	6.20	6.73
5	1	Citi	6.16	10.74
6	6	HSBC	5.58	4.99
7	8	Goldman Sachs	5.53	4.43
8	5	Deutsche Bank	5.41	5.68
9	9	Standard Chartered	4.49	4.26
10	11	State Street	4.37	3.36

Source: *Euromoney* 2018

and cooperated with one another has many of the characteristics seen in the foreign exchange and Libor rate scandals, including the use of electronic chat rooms.

If one looks at the global derivatives markets, the picture becomes even more concentrated. According to data from the U.S. Comptroller of the Currency, there are six banks—JPMorgan, Citibank, Goldman Sachs, Bank of America, HSBC and Wells Fargo—that control well over 90% of all trading in over-the-counter (OTC) interest rate derivates in the first quarter of 2018, a percentage that has remained relatively constant.[4] The dominance of these organizations across global capital markets cannot be understated. Why is this important in terms of our discussion on culture and conduct? As we have seen in the Libor and foreign exchange scandals, the individuals involved in these markets tend to know one another quite well. They often move from bank to bank, and are knitted together both professionally and socially. They also have common clients, who can be at a disadvantage given the enormous influence these institutions have in the pricing of products, whether in fixed-income, currencies or derivatives. With such power and dominance, there is always the risk that the customer's interests may be less than foremost in the minds of those servicing their financial needs.

How that comes about, and whether the mammoth size of these institutions plays a role in fostering such behavior, is an important question to consider. Institutional size, concentration and complexity may ultimately lie among the root causes of the misconduct and unethical practices that have been unearthed.

The Bigness Crisis

The consolidation of America's financial services industry is not a new phenomenon. It has its roots in the 1970s and 1980s as deregulation led banks to gradually wade into other forms of business, outside the traditional activities of deposit taking and lending. Much of this shift has been documented in the growth of noninterest income as a prime source of revenue versus more traditional interest income from lending. Noninterest income can be broadly defined as income from services that generate fees, such as trading. By 2001, noninterest income accounted for 43% of net operating revenue among U.S. banks, up sharply from only 25% in 1984.[5] During the 1980s, for example, commercial banks ventured into the business of creating and trading asset-backed securities. With large portfolios of loans on their books, banks, taking a page from their securities industry brethren—such as Salomon Brothers, one of the early innovators—bundled their loan portfolios in automobiles, for example, and sold them as attractive-yielding securities. This was new terrain for commercial banks that were federally insured. Deregulation allowed the banks to grow their capital market activities organically and expand their revenue base outside of wholesale lending, consumer and corporate banking. But the major milestone, opening the floodgates toward greater concentration, was abandonment of the Great Depression Era Glass–Steagall Act in 1999, which had kept banks from directly entering the securities business. "At the time, official supervisors and regulators did not seem to grasp the ramifications – from risk contagion to conflicts of interest – of lowering the firewalls between financial sectors," notes economist Henry Kaufman in *Tectonic Shifts in Financial Markets*.[6] The impact on institutional size and industry concentration was considerable. As recently as 1990, the ten largest financial companies held about 10% of U.S. financial assets. By 2016 they held about 80%. During this transition, many of what were the largest firms and banks on Wall Street disappeared through mergers and acquisitions. Looking at the fifteen largest U.S. institutions in 1991, all but five have lost their independence, as they were merged in those remaining survivors. Investment banking, what was once a domain of private partnerships, is now run mostly by corporate entities. Only two organizations from that period—Goldman Sachs and Morgan Stanley—remain independent, however, both became bank holding companies during the crisis of 2008 in order to survive. As Kaufman observes, the consequences of financial concentration have been several, not least is a correlation between organizational size and rule breaking. Evidence gathered by the CCP Research Foundation (UK) found that in the period 2010–2015 one-sixteenth of the world's largest lenders incurred more than $300 billion in fines, settlements, and provisions related to financial wrongdoing. In its most recent analysis, the group reported that for the five-year rolling period (2012–2016) 20 of the world's largest banks incurred so-called "conduct costs" totaling over of £264 billion, a 32.0% increase when compared with the first five-year period (2008–2012). A comparison of the banks cited in the foundation's latest report with the banks listed in the *Euromoney* foreign exchange table shows an unsurprising similarity. Does institutional size, then, play a role in misconduct? "Much of this troubling record, it seems to me, stems from the conflicts of interest inherent in financial conglomerates that too often operate on both sides of trades and offer consulting and auditing services to their clients," writes Kaufman. While many of the largest banks argue that scale enables them to better serve their global clients, there would also appear to be a reduction in competition among those in the upper echelons. "The cost of convenience for financial markets is diminished competitiveness," writes Kaufman. Less competition can come about in several ways, with the most pernicious and destructive being when banks conspire to manipulate markets for their own benefit.

Compositional Change: Growth of Transactional Model

An important by-product of lowering the barriers that separated commercial banking from the securities business and other forms of riskier, more highly-leveraged activities, was the effect it had on the customer. Banking gradually moved from a "relationship model," where client interests, and importantly client contact, was paramount, to a "transactional model" where clients became more like a counterparty, someone at the other end of the phone, or a symbol on an electronic screen. (The term "transactional model" is used here to describe the increased growth of trading and sales as a source of revenue from clients. Transaction banking is also used to describe other services, such as cash management, that banks offer their clients.) The relative decline of the relationship model has also affected the volatility of bank earnings. Bank loans are inherently more relationship based and therefore have higher "switching costs" versus fee-based activities such as trading. Fee-based activities also tend to require greater leverage, making bank earnings more susceptible to large swings in revenue.[7] As fee-based or transactional activities became more the norm, distance grew between the bank and client. This distance was a contributing factor to the changed nature of the relationship between the two, and helped to facilitate the type of behavior toward customers that would have previously been limited, or constrained.

In a pure transactional model, all parties are supposedly acting with the same set of information. In theory, so-called "perfect information" prohibits any party to a transaction to have an unfair advantage, and who can thereby extract a more favorable price from the other party. By contrast, a relationship model, or what some might call a "trust-based" model, operates where there is less than perfect information, or where information is more difficult to obtain or quantify. An example would be the classic role played by investment banks in bringing private companies to market—the initial public offering process. Because the firms vying for an IPO are private, there is limited information about them for the public to view or investigate. The value provided by the investment bank is in performing this due diligence by meeting with the private firm, reviewing its books and records, its operating model, its financing, and overall longer term business plans. In other words, the investment bank is acting as a "trusted" advisor to its clients when it suggests that an investment in the IPO might be worthwhile. The reputation of the trusted advisor develops over long periods of time, and this is still the case in investment banking today, where the relationship between client and customer is more intimate due to the nature of the business.

But as the business model of large financial firms evolved toward trading and sales operations, the role of a trusted advisor has become less important; presumably, both sides in a dollar-euro foreign exchange trade, for example, see where the price is currently being offered and understand the reasons why. Of course, in the real world, as we have seen, there is less than perfect information in such markets. The buyer and seller are often not on an even informational-playing field. Those making markets across various asset classes often have a competitive advantage simply because they have better information, an advantage that becomes exacerbated when market makers decide to collude or conspire against their clients.

Bigness Breeds Silos

The enormity of today's modern banks has also led to the creation of multiple organizations within the larger sphere that have their own business mandates, clients, and are run almost autonomously from the rest of the organization. As Gillian Tett notes in *The Silo Effect*, when she tried to get at the roots of the financial crisis she found many examples of silos within institutions that ran to their own tune. "[A]lmost everywhere I looked in the financial crisis it seemed that tunnel vision and tribalism had contributed to the disaster. People were trapped inside their little specialist departments, social groups, teams, or pockets of knowledge. Or, it might be said, inside their silos."[8]

We have seen how silos insulated themselves within organizations during the Libor and foreign exchange scandals. Employees in these trading groups had their own language and culture that transcended the larger corporate entity, and because of legal constraints which made it difficult for banks to document their misconduct when fired, many remained in the industry. "(This is a) confederation of individuals who know each other well, and are able to move from institution to institution and keep doing business with their brothers and comrades, and this causes some real problems," said Thomas Baxter, former general counsel of the Federal Reserve Bank of New York at a Thomson Reuters conference in 2016.[9]

One might argue that the Goldman Abacus deal was also driven in part by a sub-culture that viewed the publicly stated values and principles of the firm as little more than official window dressing. These silos have arisen in part due to the continued specialized nature of finance, and along with it growing complexity. Where traditional finance might have allowed a young individual to start working in one part of the organization, gain proficiency and then move to different businesses, today, that type of career path is now virtually closed off. The complex nature of the various businesses housed within the silos of large financial firms requires specialized knowledge, acquired over years of hands-on experience and training, making most employees only valuable to an organization for what they are currently doing. Should that activity cease to be a profitable line of business, whether due to changing market conditions or the continued advance of technology, the employee becomes expendable, as their skill sets are no longer of value or relevant. A clear example can be seen in today's fixed-income markets, where client interaction via salespeople was once a key component of the business model. Today, with increased automation and electronic trading, the need for individuals to "get on the phone" with a client has diminished. Those who performed this task over most of their careers now face an unenviable future of trying to apply their sales skills in other industries. Many have left the financial sector altogether.

As the nature of finance becomes more complex, so do the skill requirements. Young recruits coming out of college today have a much higher proficiency in technical skills, whether in software, analytics or algorithmic development, a reflection of how the business has evolved. It has been well-documented how some of the largest banks on Wall Street have teams of individuals with advanced degrees in computer science and disciplines that are well outside of what one would consider finance. And as the pace of specialization continues to grow, the language, norms, and cultures of these businesses will become even more difficult to penetrate from the outside, which, in turn, will make management of these businesses more challenging, requiring individuals who have deep knowledge and specialized expertise. A study by researchers at Indiana University's Kelley School of Business found that in the decade leading up the 2008 crisis, the financial services sector attracted many top graduates in engineering and computer science, with approximately 10% moving into finance within five years of graduation. A big attraction, says the study, was the higher compensation finance offered than had the graduates founded their own companies with innovative patents.[10]

Meanwhile, a separate analysis suggested JPMorgan's Asia Pacific Unit was targeting a higher proportion of engineering, neuroscience and psychology graduates versus those from traditional business schools, a reflection of the changing nature of their business.[11]

Managing Diverse Cultures

All of which begs the question: are today's financial organizations too large to manage? And are the numerous cultures that arise within the different business silos too distinct to meld into a common culture, with well-defined shared values and ethics? "I think it's hard to be identified with a firm that's very, very large," said William Dudley, president of the Federal Reserve Bank of New York, in an interview for this book in early 2018. "There has been research on the optimal group size and once you get beyond a certain point it breaks down in terms of identity and it's about 300 people. You can see how that could work pretty well on a trading desk, but it doesn't work very well in a firm that has several hundred thousand people."

Dudley, who retired in June 2018, and has been one of the most outspoken regulators on culture and conduct, said that one of the puzzling aspects of the cultural breakdown seen at banks was that some of the largest scandals had their origins in London. One theory, he suggested, is that cultural norms within British banking institutions underwent a significant upheaval after the so-called "Big Bang," a term used to describe the abrupt deregulation of financial markets in the City in 1986. The shift included the abolition of fixed commission charges, and distinction between stockjobbers and stockbrokers on the London Stock Exchange. In addition, the markets underwent a change from open-outcry to electronic, screen-based trading. The overhaul of the City's established ways took place under Prime Minister Margaret Thatcher. What also emerged during the period was an influx of U.S. financial institutions, many of whom acquired long-established British banks and organizations. The cultural impact of the American takeover is something that might have simmered below the surface for many of those working in the industry.

"Now the people are working for an American institution, or a foreign banking institution, and don't really have that much identity - almost like a 'gun for hire,'" said Dudley. "I think that's one aspect: how do you get people to identify with a firm and not just their professional 'tribe'. The second question is how does a firm maintain a set of values that speaks to the multitude of people across the firm?"

As already noted, many of the largest financial firms have large and diverse business units that are run in a relatively independent fashion. The nature of the work can often be very different, requiring employees with different skills sets as well as personalities. We've often heard the term "cultural fit" used to describe how prospective employees are evaluated when applying for a position. Cultural fit can mean displaying a set of personal interests, habits and ways of communicating that are distinct from whether you can do the job. "I know you can do the job, but I'm not sure if you're the right fit for this role" can mean many things, but often what the manager is really saying is that he or she doesn't see you fitting in *culturally*; they have a gut instinct, or first impression that says "this person is competent and experienced enough, but I don't see him as a part of our team." Having the right cultural makeup for a job in private banking will be very different from a role in spot FX trading, for instance. This might seem obvious, but when trying to understand whether such organizations can develop a common culture that is embraced by all employees across different businesses, not to mention different geographic regions, the challenges of accomplishing that goal becomes very apparent. Where does an employee's loyalty lie? To the business unit they work for, or the firm? How are they evaluated and compensated, and by whom? If one begins to ask these questions, it becomes clear that there is no simple way to instill a common set of values and ethics across a large and diverse organization. We will get into how such challenges might be addressed by middle and senior managers, compliance and human resource staff, but acknowledging that organizational size is a large hurdle in the culture battle is critical in developing a better understanding of how to get to the root causes of the conduct problem. Whether organizational size becomes a problem too far remains unclear, but as Dudley suggests, one needs to engage the issue. "Fundamentally, are these firms just too large and complex to manage properly? The question that is on the table, that people should perhaps think about, is whether this is just sort of mission impossible in the sense that we are asking people to do things that are just not possible given the scale and complexity (of their organizations)."

Organizational size undoubtedly is a factor in the debate over conduct and culture. It has implications in how the fiduciary role banks play for their customers is affected, particularly when there is increased pressure to drive products and sales under a transactional business model. Size and concentration, and the silo-ed nature of businesses, can also make it easier for banks to collude and manipulate markets and defraud customers. Lastly, managing large, complex institutions may be a challenge beyond the scope and abilities of senior management. Where there are diverse and unique sub-cultures, where employees often align themselves with the values and behaviors of their teams and co-workers, it becomes much harder to define and instill a shared purpose with common values across the organization. At what institutional size does the challenge to create a common culture become greater than management's capabilities? There is, of course, no clear answer. All that one can say is that it is much easier to align your employees around a coherent cultural framework when you are a smaller organization. "The task of engaging with our people on cultural norms and behavior is operationally easier to do if you're a firm with 5000 people than if you have 30,000 people," said Stephen Scherr, a senior Goldman Sachs executive in a 2018 interview.[12] Such a reality should not mean that these behemoth institutions should not try to instill strong ethics and strive for a healthy culture. They must do. It is only to recognize how much harder and longer the path may be. Indeed, it is likely to remain a never-ending road, replete with detours and an ever-changing landscape.

Notes

1. Euromoney FX Survey 2018: https://www.euromoney.com/Media/documents/euromoney/pdf/Euromoney-FX-Survey-2018-Press-Release.pdf.
2. Federal Reserve Bank of New York Primary Dealer Statistics: https://www.newyorkfed.org/medialibrary/media/banking/reportingforms/primarystats/msytdpdf.pdf?la=en.
3. "Goldman, Other Big Banks Secretly Used Chat Rooms to Rig U.S. Treasury Auctions, Lawsuit Alleges," Kevin Dugan, *New York Post*, November 16, 2017.
4. Office of the Comptroller of the Currency, Quarterly Report on Bank Trading and Derivatives Activities, First Quarter 2018.

5. "Diversification in Banking—Is Noninterest Income the Answer?" Kevin J. Stiroh, Federal Reserve Bank of New York, September 23, 2002.
6. *Tectonic Shifts in Financial Markets*, Henry Kaufman, Palgrave Macmillan, 2016.
7. "Noninterest Income and Financial Performance at U.S. Commercial Banks," Robert DeYoung and Tara Rice, Federal Reserve Bank of Chicago, August 2003.
8. *The Silo Effect: The Peril of Expertise and the Promise of Breaking Down Barriers*, Gillian Tett, Simon & Schuster, 2016.
9. "Progress, but Not yet Victory, in Banking System Culture," Henry Engler and Thomson Reuters, Regulatory Intelligence, June 17, 2016.
10. "Superstar (and Entrepreneurial) Engineers in Finance Jobs," Nandini Gupta and Isaac Hacamo, Kelley School of Business, Indiana University, March 2018.
11. "Wall Street's Biggest Bank Hires More Than Just Business Majors," Cathy Chan, Bloomberg, March 28, 2018.
12. "EXCLUSIVE: Goldman's Blankfein Enlists Senior Management in Conduct, Culture Initiative," Henry Engler, *Reuters*, May 16, 2018.

4

Global Regulators: Limits on What They Can Do

Regulators are always a step behind the industries they oversee. This is just as true for oil and gas as it is for financial services. The nature of their function and role makes it inherent that they are reactive to events as they unfold, and the new regulations or rules that typically follow are reflective of what was perceived to have gone wrong. With culture and conduct issues regulators are finding themselves on different and uncertain terrain, recognizing there are limits to what they can do given the nature of the underlying problems. On the one hand, they need to be vocal—which they have been. Not a month goes by without a senior regulator in the USA, UK, or Asia, voicing the need for banks to do more to curb bad behavior. While many believe progress has been made in the aftermath of the crisis, more recent developments, in particular, the Wells Fargo fake accounts episode, highlight the need to remain vigilant.

Yet unlike other areas of supervision and rule-making, culture and conduct are more difficult to prescribe. There is no easy or common definition of what constitutes a good or ethical culture. Some U.S. regulators—taking a page from Justice Potter Stewart's infamous remark on defining pornography—"I know it when I see it."—have noted that they can sense by spending time in an organization whether it has a strong cultural framework. But they are still reluctant to provide a tool-kit of suggestions on how to improve internal practices. "While we might provide a view on things they might be able to do better, we don't have an official assessment process for whether a cultural program or anything like that is appropriate or not. We focus more on how well have the expected behaviors been articulated, communicated and whether people are following them," Molly Scherf, a senior official at the

Office of the Comptroller of the Currency, told a Thomson Reuters forum on bank culture reform in 2016.[1] Scherf's views are shared by others who recognize that unlike most forms of risk in the organizations they oversee, one cannot put a quantifiable metric or measure around conduct or culture; there is no comparable "culture at risk" yardstick that one can use to indicate whether an organization is more, or less prone to bad behavior, more, or less ethical in terms of its engagement with clients. Martin Wheatley, former head of the UK's Financial Conduct Authority, told a Thomson Reuters conference in early 2018 that conduct is not an issue that one can wrap rules around.[2] "The problem with culture is that it's not about compliance. It's a value, not a rule," said Wheatley. "Culture is not a rulebook, it's a set of values… I do think that this is one of the big problems." Regulators have come to recognize they cannot enforce good cultures through their supervisory process, and even if they could, a rule-based, prescriptive approach would likely backfire. Why? Because banks would then abide by those rules like any other regulation, and when exam time comes around demonstrate to the regulator they have ticked all the boxes on the cultural and conduct checklist. As much as banks would prefer that type of oversight—in common with other forms of quantifiable financial risk; credit or liquidity risk, for example—regulators have come to understand that moving toward a quantifiable approach for such issues is self-defeating; one cannot get to the bottom of a firm's conduct and culture problems by creating metrics that allows one to measure whether you are being effective or not. That's not to say there isn't a role for analytics and other forms of technology in addressing misconduct. A whole cottage industry has developed around providing services that use sophisticated tools, such as machine learning and artificial intelligence, to monitor employee behavior, with the hope of potentially heading off bad or harmful decisions. But there is a distinction—and here guidance from regulators becomes critical in using technology to mitigate risk that may emanate from bad behavior versus getting to the root causes of why otherwise good employees make bad decisions. Many firms may believe that one way to appease their regulator is to demonstrate they have an army of technologists building sophisticated monitoring and surveillance tools that alert compliance and control staff in advance of when an employee might be putting the organization at risk. But one needs to be cognizant of the fact that such tools are more a form of risk management than cultural or behavioral reform. "I think it's perfectly sensible to do those kinds of things because there are going to be bad actors, and prudent risk management is that you want to make sure you are aware," said Dudley. "But I don't think that regime in any way helps you build better conduct or culture. It helps you root out bad actors a little bit sooner, but I don't think it helps your broad culture." Moreover, if a bank relies on such tools, believing that it will lead to a stronger culture, the reverse may come about. "People may experience it as there is a presumption that the firm thinks there are lots of bad actors in the organization and they are trying to prevent them from doing bad things. That doesn't seem to lead to a very good culture," said Dudley.

Principles Instead of Rules

When regulators talk about conduct and culture they often speak about "principles" instead of rules, again recognizing that one cannot quantify culture in the same way as with other forms of financial service activities. A principles-based approach toward conduct will mean, however, that you are limited in what you can do as a regulator in addressing issues that you see arise in the industry. As Andrew Bailey, current head of the UK's FCA said in 2018 speech: "Culture is not naturally pursued by a regulator like the FCA by making rules. We would not achieve much by making a rule which said that all firms should have a good culture. I want to be clear however … that culture in firms is influenced by the rules we make and the incentives they create, so there is a very important role for our rules, but it is not a direct prescribing of culture."[3] In other words, regulators can indirectly influence culture and behavior by implementing rules in other areas. (Bailey cites rules on compensation as one such indirect influencer.) Banks, on the other hand, realizing there are no specific "red lines" around conduct and culture, also struggle to better understand what regulators are looking for when they evaluate organizations. The lack of clarity regarding the rules of the road therefore makes the interplay between banks and regulators more of a "learn as go" process, with efforts by the latter to coax, nudge, and push the industry toward doing things they might not have otherwise done on their own. Perhaps a good example of such cajoling is the UK's Banking Standards Board (BSB), an organization created in 2015. A private industry body, funded with member subscriptions, and open to all bank and building societies in the UK, the organization is neither a regulator nor trade association. It has no statutory powers, and doesn't speak for or lobby for the industry. While the BSB is touted as an industry initiative, its roots sprouted in the wake of the scandals in the City of London, with a parliamentary commission launched to investigate the causes. The commission's recommendations, many of which focused on conduct and cultural failings at the largest banks, included the creation of an industry-led board that would implement enhanced standards through a voluntary code of practice. The seven largest

UK banks were at the creation of the board, with a former senior UK Treasury official, Alison Cottrell, appointed as its head. Perhaps the most widely read of the Banking Standard Board's output is its annual industry review of behavior, competence, and culture in UK banking. The review, which surveys banks across the country, is viewed as a barometer of how they are doing in their conduct and culture efforts. The most recent assessment for 2017 suggests much more work is needed. From the more than 36,000 employees at 25 banks and building societies surveyed, more than a quarter believed their job is damaging their health and wellbeing, and a similar proportion are afraid of negative consequences if they speak up about concerns. "This is a mixture of fear that they will get into trouble and futility that it will serve no useful purpose," said Dame Colette Bowe, who chairs the BSB.[4]

U.S. regulators have said a similar standards board and industry review process might be useful for American banks. "There are members of the UK standards board that are U.S. firms, and if they start to see that there is actually value to them, then I think that will prompt others," said Dudley of the New York Fed. But as with any industry initiative there is a collective action problem. No bank wishes to go first and lead such projects unless they believe they have support from others. How that support develops may ultimately require stronger nudging by regulators. Even in the UK, the BSB, while touted as an industry-led group, was heavily influenced by regulators who argued for such a body. Regulators have influence in such areas, but how they pick and choose when to act, and what to prescribe remains difficult. It might well be that a similar standards body emerges for U.S. banks, however, much will depend on who the regulatory actors are and the appetite for such an organization among banking leaders. Dudley, who retired in mid-2018, and was replaced by former San Francisco Federal Reserve Bank president John Williams, made conduct and culture a priority under his reign. It remains to be seen how closely Williams follows suit.

Executive Accountability: UK Senior Managers Regime

Another effort by UK authorities that might be closer to a rules than principles-based approach was the establishment of the Senior Managers Regime in 2015. The basic principle of the regulation is that of responsibility and accountability. A senior manager has to take responsibility for the activities under their control. Likewise, they should be held accountable for that responsibility. Individual executive accountability has been a sore point leading up to and since the financial crisis. As many have lamented, few, if any executives have gone to jail or been severely penalized for wrongdoings that happened on their watch. The counter to this rests with the tenets of criminal law; specifically, that to send someone to jail one needs to prove criminal intent, not an easy task when considering large, diverse, complex financial organizations, where senior executives are several steps removed from those committing malfeasance. What did they know and when did they know it becomes much harder for prosecutors to nail down in cases where there are several lines of authority. What the Senior Managers Regime tries to do is make the accountability and responsibility trail more specific, requiring key individuals in the firm to be identified and held responsible for misconduct under their command. By identifying individuals with specific roles and responsibilities, and documenting them explicitly, the hope is to prompt managers to keep a closer eye on what their employees are doing. Whether a similar regime might work in the United States is open to question.

Another component of the UK's approach has been executive remuneration. The term that Bailey of the FCA likes to use is "skin in the game" for those running the shop, or putting a significant part of variable executive compensation at risk over future years. In practice, this means devising policies that require deferred compensation over a period of time, and backing up those policies up with so-called 'malus' and 'clawback' rules. Put simply, malus occurs when the deferred but unvested remuneration is taken back by the organization because of misconduct, wrongdoing, or problem discovered at the firm. Clawback is pretty much the same, except that it involves taking back compensation after it has been paid out. What indirect influence does Bailey and the FCA hope to achieve with such rules? "I think that deferral of vesting of remuneration achieves some of the incentive effects of the old partnership structure, in the sense that both create skin in the game. For partners, this meant leaving equity capital in the firm. This system died out as the major firms grew rapidly and needed to raise capital on a scale which went beyond the resources of partners," said Bailey. Many industry observers have pointed to earlier partnership models as a restraining influence on bad behavior, with the personal, financial risk of the partners incentivizing them to keep a watchful eye on employees and business practices. Dudley also sees benefits in considering creative ways of compensating senior management, and believes that putting executives on the hook for a portion of the fines a firm might have to pay yielding similar benefits. "I suspect changes in these areas would lead senior managers to encourage their staff to speak up earlier about emerging risks, be more attentive when red flags were raised, and respond sooner and more forcefully," said Dudley at a U.S. Chamber of

Commerce event in early 2018.[5] Still, there is the looming collective action problem. It would be difficult to imagine any one institution putting in place such a radical overhaul of their compensation scheme whereby senior management had to pay for a portion of their firm's fines. To do so might risk a flight of their most talented executives—or at least that would be the common argument. A possible counter argument could be that such a first-mover would attract individuals who are unafraid of taking on such a challenge; that by senior management having more financial "skin in the game" they will attract others who share their values and ethics. And, if one truly believes that ethical cultures make good business sense, then the payoff in the form of longer-term financial success would surely follow.

In his book on Goldman's organizational drift, Mandis pointed to a proposal made by Peter Weinberg, the grandson of senior partner Sidney Weinberg, in a *Wall Street Journal* article in 2009. Weinberg argued that people who manage trading or the asset management business should have some of their own capital at stake. Such a requirement would "better align the pocketbooks of Wall Street with the pocketbooks of financial markets and our economy," said Weinberg. Mandis himself argues that such a "partnership plan" might lead those running Goldman and similar organizations "to place a greater emphasis on the whole enterprise than on themselves or their group. Financial interdependence and personal liability … might make risk management and ethical standards a higher priority and reemphasize a social network of trust…"

"Rolling Bad Apples"

The way in which bad behavior is described on Wall Street has evolved over time. We have, for example, the "rogue" trader, someone with seemingly sinister intentions, who seeks to profit by exploiting weaknesses in a bank's internal controls. When things turn sour, the "rogue" then tries to cover up his trail of losses, in some cases leading to catastrophic consequences. Several rogue traders have in the past gone to jail, or been heavily fined. Nick Leeson, a former derivatives broker, who in the 1990s engaged in fraudulent, unauthorized speculative trading, is now frequently cited as the first rogue trader. Leeson's trading activities led to the collapse of Barings Bank, the UK's oldest merchant bank. By using fake accounts, Leeson covered up his massive losses while working for Barings in Singapore. His losses totaled $1.4 billion, twice the bank's available trading capital. After his fraud was uncovered, he fled the country and later arrested in Frankfurt in November 1995.

He pleaded guilty to two counts of "deceiving the bank's auditors and of cheating the Singapore exchange," including forging documents. Leeson spent six and a half years in Singapore prison, and during that time published an autobiography called, *Rogue Trader*.[6]

More recently, Jerome Kerviel, a trader for the French bank Societe Generale, was convicted in 2008 for initiating equity derivatives trades totaling €50 billion, far in excess of his authorized limits. It cost the bank €4.9 billion to unwind the transactions. Kerviel started his career in the bank's compliance function, and then moved into the equity derivatives. The bank claimed Kerviel "had taken massive fraudulent directional positions in 2007 and 2008 far beyond his limited authority." While he did not profit personally, Kerviel said his actions were designed to increase the bank's profits and that others were well aware of his actions. In 2010, Kerviel served just five months of a three-year sentence, and in 2016 a French court slashed the damages Kerviel owed the bank from an initial €4.9 billion to €1 million. The court also said that while Kerviel was "partially liable" for the losses that nearly destroyed Societe Generale in 2008, the "patchy nature" of the bank's control systems limited its rights to damages.[7]

Traders such as Kerviel and Leeson lie at the extreme end of bad behavior, which in the latter's case prompted the collapse a major bank. There are many others in the industry, who while less threatening, nonetheless pose risks to the organizations they work for. So-called "rolling bad apples," these individuals move from firm to firm, often dismissed because of some wrongdoing detected by their employer. As we saw in the foreign exchange market scandal, the businesses units within these organizations are tightly-knit, with many employees having come to know one another through past working associations. This cultural bond and network become very valuable when one is looking for a new position. For regulators, the problem is that when an employee leaves a firm due to some form of bad behavior, the details and circumstances of the departure are kept confidential and cannot be divulged to any future employer. A person who was let go from "Bank A" for some trading violation, for example, will use his network of friends to find a new job. If he gets an interview at "Bank B" the hiring manager will not have the details of dismissal from "Bank A," thereby improving his chances of returning to the industry.

In certain jurisdictions, there are mechanisms by which "rolling bad apples" are kept track of. In a 2018 report, the Financial Stability Board highlighted a range of different approaches used by regulators.[8] For example, in Germany, the primary financial regulator, BaFin, operates an internal employee and complaints register tracking an individual's misbehavior.

When certain individuals seek to move from one investment firm to another, BaFin can use the information in the register to consider whether it should prohibit the firm's employment of such individuals. Meanwhile, in Japan, the Securities Dealers Association has rules under which its members must inform the association about "inappropriate acts" that employees have committed. When a member firm intends to hire a person, it must inquire with the association whether that person has committed an inappropriate act. The association will then reply based on the record of inappropriate acts it keeps. The association can also prohibit firms from hiring persons for a certain period of time, if the act committed by them is considered to impair public confidence in the industry.

The Swiss Financial Market Supervisor Authority (FINMA) has two tools it uses in its oversight process. First, is a nonpublic database of individuals with questionable business conduct or with a track record of not meeting relevant legal requirements. The purpose of the database is to ensure that only people who meet the proper business conduct requirements are involved in the strategic or executive management of authorized institutions or hold qualified participations in them. Second, FINMA sends a business conduct letter to those entered on the watch list in certain circumstances, including where there is a possibility of the individual assuming a position subject to business conduct requirements in the future. While the business conduct letter is not a ruling, it will inform the individual that FINMA reserves the right to review compliance with business conduct requirements if the individual intends to assume a specific position.

In the United Kingdom, references need to be prepared by the firm using a mandated template with which they must then share certain information about employees moving between firms. The purpose is to assist companies in assessing whether a new hire is "fit and proper." The information is expected to include any breaches of regulatory requirements, internal disciplinary actions, and breaches of the FCA's individual conduct rules. The references, which include six years of the employee's employment history, are required for anyone performing a senior manager, nonexecutive director or significant harm function.

In the United States, however, the only registry similar to those described is maintained by the Financial Industry Regulatory Authority (FINRA), which has a publicly available database of brokers in the securities industry called BrokerCheck. The database contains background information for every registered firm and broker including: the person's current employer; qualifications, including examination history; registration history; employment history; other business activities; and disclosure events in the person's past, such as law enforcement actions (whether civil or criminal) and customer disputes. However, for the U.S. banking sector no comparable database exists. Therefore, in the foreign exchange market, individuals who have been let go from a bank because of some wrongdoing, can move to another bank without the future employer's knowledge of past behavior. The same holds true in other areas of banking. Regulators, such as Dudley at the New York Fed, have argued for several years for the banking industry to consider adopting such a tool. It remains to be seen whether such a registry will come about, and at least for now there doesn't appear to be much industry support.

"When I look at the U.S. versus the UK, I feel that the U.S. has not gone as far the UK has in terms of standardized evaluations, in terms of dealing with the rolling bad apple problem," said Dudley in the interview.

Which brings us back to how far regulators might push the envelope for actions they deem desirable to curb bad conduct.

Limits to Regulatory Patience

It has been made clear by various regulatory bodies that culture and conduct are areas of supervision better governed by principles than rules, and that banks themselves should know best how to instill ethical behavior across their businesses. Still, we are beginning to see evidence that there are limits to what regulators will tolerate. In the United States, the Federal Reserve took unprecedented action in early 2018 against Wells Fargo by issuing a "cease and desist" order, putting a temporary halt to the bank's business expansion plans. The Fed, frustrated over the lack of progress Wells Fargo made in addressing inadequate controls and safeguards over its consumer business following the fake accounts scandal, put curbs on the bank's ability to expand its business until it remedied numerous failures found by the regulator.

"We cannot tolerate pervasive and persistent misconduct at any bank and the consumers harmed by Wells Fargo expect that robust and comprehensive reforms will be put in place to make certain that the abuses do not occur again," Chair Janet L. Yellen said. "The enforcement action we are taking today will ensure that Wells Fargo will not expand until it is able to do so safely and with the protections needed to manage all of its risks and protect its customers."

In addition to the growth restriction, the Fed's order required the bank to improve its governance and risk management processes, including strengthening the effectiveness of oversight by its board of directors. Until the bank makes sufficient improvements, it will be restricted from growing any larger than its total asset size as of the end of 2017. The Fed required each current director to sign the cease and desist order. In its statement, the regulator said: "Wells Fargo pursued a business strategy that prioritized its overall growth without ensuring appropriate management of all key risks. The firm did not have an effective firm-wide risk management framework in place that covered all key risks. This prevented the proper escalation of serious compliance breakdowns to the board of directors."

Underscoring its frustration, the Fed also sent letters to each current Wells Fargo board member confirming that the firm's board of directors, during the period of compliance breakdowns, did not meet supervisory expectations. Letters were also sent to former Chairman and Chief Executive Officer John Stumpf, and past lead independent director Stephen Sanger, stating that their performance did not meet the Federal Reserve's expectations. The Fed's action stunned the U.S. banking community. Many viewed the order as a warning shot to other banks who fail to fix problems in a timely manner. It also highlighted how a firm's cultural and ethical lapses, in this case the widespread opening of fake retail customer accounts, can have costly business implication outside the areas where remediation is required. The unilateral action by the Fed also suggests that the regulator does not have unlimited patience with banks when addressing major lapses in risk management and business oversight. This lesson is one that banks will need to bear in mind over the coming years, particularly should new evidence emerge over unethical behavior or misconduct on a par with Wells Fargo. And in the Wells case, the Fed's action showed it is demanding greater accountability and oversight from the boards of such large institutions. The Fed's action also suggests that such organizations need to go beyond what they might think is acceptable in remedying faults in their organization. In the February 2018 interview with Dudley of the New York Fed, the regulator suggested that for some organizations the job may be too difficult, leaving the Fed with few options.

"If the choices are you either get to fix your culture and continue at your current scale, or you don't fix your culture and we actually have to scale you down to size, I think they are going to – again, this is about incentives – take culture a lot more seriously. And there is a pretty existential consequence of not fixing this …"

Another recent example of regulatory intervention, this time in the United Kingdom, involved Jes Staley, chief executive of Barclays bank, and the action by the FCA and the Bank of England's Prudential Regulation Authority (PRA) against Staley for his efforts to uncover an internal whistleblower. In May 2018, regulators fined Staley £642,430—representing just

14% of his total compensation—for trying to uncover the identity of an anonymous whistleblower. The investigation by the FCA and PRA was the first public probe by the regulators under the new "senior managers" regime designed to improve accountability. The decision means that Staley becomes the first chief executive of a major financial institution to be fined by the financial regulators and keep his job.

What the regulators concluded from the investigation is that Staley, an ex-JPMorgan executive, "breached the standard of care required and expected of a chief executive in a way that risked undermining confidence in Barclays' whistleblowing procedures." said an official from the FCA.[9] "Whistleblowers play a vital role in exposing poor practice and misconduct in the financial services sector. It is critical that individuals are able to speak up anonymously and without fear of retaliation if they want to raise concerns." However, some industry observers said the FCA's lack of stronger action was a missed opportunity. Specifically, the regulators found that under the senior managers regime Staley was in breach of Individual Conduct Rule 2 (the requirement to act with due skill, care, and diligence), but crucially the regulators said he had not acted with a lack of integrity. If he had been guilty of the latter he would have found himself in possible violation of the FCA's so-called "fit and proper person test" under the new regime. Not everyone agreed. Some critics argued that the FCA's decision showed there were special rules for people who run large banks, and different rules for others.

Staley's troubles, however, are not over. New York's Department of Financial Services is still investigating the incident and has yet to publish its findings. The New York regulator is known for being very tough on banks and their managers, and has jurisdiction over Barclays given its New York presence. Moreover, given the increased attention paid to whistleblowers in the United States, particularly in cases of sexual misconduct and abuse, there might be less tolerance for a bank chief executive seeking to unmask those who are concerned with behavior they believe is at odds with the ethics and culture of an organization.

What the Fed's action against Wells Fargo and the Staley case demonstrate is that regulators have rules in place that can be enforced to effect cultural change. Some of these rules are new, as in the UK's senior managers regime, others, such as "cease and desist" orders by the Fed have long been established and relate to traditional "safety and soundness" concerns. The upshot is that while financial authorities may be reluctant use such rules to punish banks or senior management when their actions are found lacking, the threat exists, which when exercised might prove effective among organizations whose commitment to cultural and ethical reform is questionable.

Notes

1. "Progress, but Not yet Victory, in Banking System Culture," Henry Engler, Thomson Reuters, Regulatory Intelligence, June 17, 2016.
2. "BANK CULTURE FORUM: Behavioral Science Gains Role as Banks Address Culture, Conduct," Henry Engler, Thomson Reuters, April 23, 2018.
3. "Transforming Culture in Financial Services," Andrew Bailey, Financial Conduct Authority, March 19, 2018.
4. "A Quarter of UK Bankers Say Their Job Is Bad for Their Health," Martin Arnold and Patrick Jenkins, *Financial Times*, March 14, 2018.
5. "The Importance of Incentives in Ensuring a Resilient and Robust Financial System," William Dudley, U.S. Chamber of Commerce, Washington, DC, March 26, 2018.
6. *Rogue Trader*, Nick Leeson (Kindle Edition), 1996, Little, Brown Book Group.
7. "Jerome Kerviel's SocGen Damages Slashed to €1m," Michael Stothard, *Financial Times*, September 23, 2016.
8. "Strengthening Governance Frameworks to Mitigate Misconduct Risks: A Toolkit for Firms and Supervisors," Financial Stability Board, April 20, 2018.
9. "FCA and PRA Jointly Fine Mr James Staley £642,430 and Announce Special Requirements Regarding Whistleblowing Systems and Controls at Barclays," Financial Conduct Authority, press release, May 5, 2018.

5

Enforcing Culture: Criminally Based Compliance

With regulators urging banks to address their culture and conduct issues, yet refraining from advancing rules or a roadmap that firms can follow and comply with, the reaction within the industry has been to take a very legalistic and, what some call, "criminally based" approach toward meeting regulatory demands. Conduct and culture issues have largely fallen within the scope of compliance and human resource functions at many organizations. These functions, particularly in compliance, are often staffed with trained lawyers, former regulators, and sometimes ex-prosecutors. (Recruitment professionals will argue, however, that more recently banks are looking for compliance professionals who have technical skills as the nature of the function has evolved.) The architecture that has arisen within the compliance function across the industry is built upon three spheres.[1] The first is education, which includes training and ensures that all employees understand the rules, laws, and code of conduct of the institution. Monitoring employees is the second sphere, which can be both direct and indirect. This type of surveillance can vary from firm-to-firm, with some organizations using very sophisticated "big data" tools and analytics to identify patterns of employee behavior that can pose risks. Direct monitoring begins at the hiring stage, where potential employees are screened for past wrongdoing, an area where U.S. regulators, as we have seen, believe more needs to be done. Indirect monitoring includes reviews of phone calls, email, and other forms of communication. In some cases, banks are now able to monitor the length of time that an employee spends at his or her desk. In addition, surveillance teams within compliance will also monitor social media for signs of behavior that could potentially put the firm at risk. The third sphere of compliance is

© The Author(s) 2018
H. Engler, *Remaking Culture on Wall Street*,
https://doi.org/10.1007/978-3-030-02086-6_5

enforcement. When spheres one and two break down, enforcement becomes the last resort with employees who have been engaged in alleged misconduct. Enforcement, of course, can take on different forms, and depends on the severity of the offense. The most extreme form is termination, which many legal experts tend to recommend—the concept of "fire quickly" is one that has become widespread, seen as a way of mitigating future risks for the organization. In cases of more serious wrongdoing, termination is only the first step on a path that can lead to cooperation with regulators and law enforcement, potential fines, debarment from the industry, loss of license, and possibly prison.

As one can see, the three spheres of compliance are very rule-based. The emphasis is on ensuring that employees understand where the "bright lines" are, and that crossing the line carries severe consequences. Since the financial crisis, and the scandals that have evolved, it would seem safe to say that the apparatus underlying the three spheres have become more invasive and pervasive for employees: the education process has increased, with more training sessions across a variety of areas where employees may come across conflict, either within the firm or with clients; the degree of monitoring has increased with the application of new technologies, such as machine learning, artificial intelligence, and the use of algorithms that can predict future behavior; and lastly, enforcement of the rules has become quicker, with many banks now adopting "zero tolerance" for those found involved in some form of misconduct. All of this has created an environment for employees where trust is at a premium, and the notion of innocent until proven guilty has been turned on its heard.

"The Surveillance State"

Widespread monitoring and surveillance of employees, an outgrowth of the criminally based approach toward compliance and advances in technology, ultimately suggests to the employee that they are not trusted; that there is a need to watch their every move for fear that they will do something that harms the organization; and that only over time might the employee establish the type of trust that comes naturally in organizations with strong ethical cultures. However, one of the important insights in behavioral economics is that people react poorly to close monitoring.[2] Heavy surveillance is a signal of distrust, which might lead to employees to engage in behaviors that are evasive, frustrating the very purpose of surveillance. As Edward Snowden has argued, heavy surveillance diminishes individual autonomy which is a cornerstone of ethical behavior. In addition, excessive surveillance could lead to reduced productivity and entrepreneurial activity.[3] Even if a large organization could achieve perfect "panopticon"—an arrangement where all employees could be observed all the time—there are some who wager that the productivity and competitive position of such firms would lag behind their peers.[4]

We need only to look outside of financial services for evidence of how pervasive monitoring of individuals often leads to behaviors that are counterproductive. When individuals know they are being watched they find ways to deal with the surveillance and circumvent the process. This doesn't necessarily mean that the intention by the individual is always to do something wrong. At a broader, societal level, the consequences of widespread monitoring can lead to behaviors that are at odds with the values of open, and democratic societies. In perhaps the grandest experiment of individual monitoring—the former German Democratic Republic—citizens were spied on by friends, neighbors, and in the worst case, their own family members. Monitoring movements and recording phone conversations were tools the intelligence services—the Ministry for State Security or State Security Service (*Staatssicherheitsdienst*), or better known as the Stasi—used in tracking individuals who posed a risk to the state.

In light of this failed social experiment, researchers have recently analyzed the consequences of the GDR's surveillance regime and found, not surprisingly, a sharp erosion of trust among those who spent much of their lives in the GDR.[5] Notably, the evidence has shown that since German reunification in 1990, interpersonal trust is lowest among those who spent their entire childhood in the GDR, and that the intention to vote and engagement with local politics is much lower in parts of the country with a "high spy density." This may help explain why more than 25 years since the GDR reunited with West Germany that many citizens in the eastern part of the German republic still feel a sense of estrangement from their western cousins. It might also have played a factor in the rise of the far-right political movement, or Alternative for Deutschland (AfD) party, which in 2017 elections won numerous seats in the country's parliament, the first time a right-wing party has entered the Bundestag in the postwar period. This illustration is merely to underscore how excessive surveillance, whether at a national level or within large organizations has limits, with the outcomes often at odds with the objectives of those in charge of the monitoring.

Within corporate compliance there are similar reasons to worry about excessive surveillance. As some legal experts have noted, compliance officials have increasingly used surveillance and monitoring to demonstrate their usefulness and value to their organizations. However, with such tools, there is the risk that they "start behaving more like cops on the beat. Although there surely is a place for such intrusion, one of the key insights of research in both behavioral economics and behavioral ethics is that monitoring intensity can backfire… Under certain circumstances, then, an increase in monitoring can actually increase misbehavior, not decrease it. One of the culture-oriented tasks for constructive compliance is explaining the presence of necessary tools in a way that is less likely to provoke dangerous reactance or demoralization, and avoiding excess."[6]

Rise of Culture Programs

It would be unfair, however, to argue that banks are solely employing surveillance and monitoring tools in their conduct and culture battles. Many institutions have in recent years delved into what culture means to their employees, and initiated enterprise-wide programs to better understand how they can develop more of a "shared-purpose" across the organization and identify problems and roadblocks to achieve such goals. At JPMorgan, for example, Sally Dewar, a managing director, described for a Thomson Reuters audience in 2016 how the bank implemented a global culture program in 2015 that included identifying 1600 so-called "cultural ambassadors," who were viewed as employees who upheld the cultural values of the firm. These ambassadors engaged approximately 16,000 employees worldwide in interviews to discover what JPMorgan's culture meant to them, what was working, and what was not.

The undertaking led to a series of reforms that were then embedded into the entire "life-cycle" of employees, from their onboarding process to performance evaluations, compensation, and any disciplinary actions that were needed.

"The way that we've thought about behavior is to look at the life cycle of an employee. From the moment that we have a recruitment campaign to inducting and onboarding that individual to training programs, to setting objectives and performance appraisals, compensation and disciplinary exits," said Dewar.

But the task of maintaining the culture program remained with the business. While compliance and human resources monitor employee behavior for any shortcomings, it is the business that owns the process, a view shared by others, said Dewar.[7]

More recently, Goldman Sachs launched a global culture and ethics training program designed for the firm's most senior executives. Led by former chief executive Lloyd Blankfein, the program, called the "Chairman's Forum," was a mandatory, global training program that convened the firm's partners and managing directors to reinforce a responsibility—particularly among the firm's leaders—for strengthening culture and reputation, according to Goldman officials.[8]

"It is critical for us as leaders to establish and maintain a culture where we ask people's opinions, help and seek out a lot of different information – a culture where people think it's not extra credit, but rather their individual responsibility, to raise issues that they are worried about," said Blankfein in a video played at the start of each session.

The program was launched in September 2017 and was expected to conclude in late 2018. It included a 2 1/2 hours session facilitated by a member of the management committee, which included Blankfein, the president and chief operating officer, division heads and a senior professional from "Pine Street," the firm's development program for partners and managing directors. Approximately 2500 of the firm's senior managers were expected to participate in the mandatory exercise. Goldman officials said a key objective of the training sessions was to make them relevant to the situations and potential conflicts the firm's managers might encounter. The fact that the sessions were facilitated by Goldman executives—as opposed to external consultants—made the programs more relevant to those who attended, they added.

In Europe, French banking giant Societe Generale launched its own "Culture & Conduct" program in 2016, aimed at building "confidence among all its stakeholders, especially its customers, and to develop the Societe Generale culture by placing values, leadership quality and behavioral integrity at the heart of its business conduct and thus achieve the highest standards of service quality, integrity and behavior," according to a description on the bank's website.[9] The bank said the program was based on the recommendations of a Group of Thirty report on bank culture, which addressed five key themes: development of the perception of culture; governance, and responsibilities of the governing bodies; performance management and incentives; staff development and training; and effectiveness of the three lines of defense.[10]

Many other large banks also now have conduct or culture officers who sit alongside senior compliance, risk management, and human resource executives. Their role is to specifically address ethical and conduct issues as they arise in the organization, as well as represent their companies in front of regulators and other bodies.

Risk Mitigation Versus Trust Building

For financial services, one needs to make a distinction between activities that are in essence "risk mitigation" versus those that help drive ethical behavior and strong cultures. There is no question that banks should apply new technologies to monitor employees to mitigate behavior that puts the organization at risk. An entire industry has been created to service the needs of these organizations, providing tools that enable firms to monitor and often predict potential fraudulent or risky behavior. Technologies such as machine learning are used to track employee interactions with colleagues and customers and identify patterns that suggest alternative objectives or potential fraud. Artificial intelligence is also being used to analyze a trader's recent trading history to spot anomalies, and in certain cases, flash a warning sign to the trader before executing another trade. There are tools that scour the metadata in email communications to understand who among a group or team of employees are considered "key influencers." At times, such individuals may not always seem to be the ones management would expect. Moreover, identifying such influencers, and whether they are in fact influential for the right reasons, is a key objective of the technology.[11] In other cases, banks are combing through vast oceans of data to simply find patterns that may prove valuable. For example, one large U.S. institution found that by examining data on when its employees entered and exited its building could predict who was about to resign from the firm. Typically, employees who are about to leave a company tend to work shorter days than normal. Once identified, these employees would be more closely monitored for any activity that suggested they are taking proprietary firm information, or passing such data to others outside the company.

All of this can be viewed as risk management or mitigation activities. They should not, however, be considered as tools to enhance ethical behavior. They might be a subset of such efforts, but to rely solely on monitoring and surveillance to limit bad behavior will get an organization only so far. Indeed, as we have seen, it could be counterproductive to lean on such techniques alone without digging deeper into how employees interact with each other and their clients, to understand their motivations and incentives, and the dynamics of the groups in which they operate. Monitoring and surveillance, and the technology that supports them, can be effective tools in spotting risky behavior early. But they need to be balanced by a more substantive understanding of group behavior, which as we will see, requires direct human intervention.

Notes

1. Haugh, Todd. (2017). "Nudging Corporate Compliance," *American Business Law Journal*, Vol. 54, Issue 4, pp. 683–741, Winter 2017.
2. Falk, Armin, and Kosfeld, Michael. (2006). "The Hidden Costs of Control," *American Economic Review*, Vol. 96, pp. 1611–1130.
3. Tenbrunsel, Ann E., and Messick, David M. (1999). "Sanctioning Systems, Decision Frames, and Cooperation," *Administrative Science Quarterly*, Vol. 44, Issue 4, pp. 684–707.
4. Langevoort, Donald C. (2002). "Monitoring: The Behavioral Economics of Corporate Compliance with Law," *Columbia Business Law Review*, Vol. 2002, p. 71.
5. Lichter, Andreas, Löffler, Max, and Siegloch, Sebastian. (2015). "The Economic Costs of Mass Surveillance: Insights from Stasi Spying in East Germany." IZA DP No. 9245.
6. Langevoort, Donald C. (2002). "Cultures of Compliance," *Georgetown University Law Center*, 2017, https://scholarship.law.georgetown.edu/facpub/1799/.
7. "Progress, But Not Yet Victory, in Banking System Culture," Henry Engler, Thomson Reuters, June 17, 2016.
8. "Exclusive: Goldman's Blankfein Enlists Senior Management in Conduct, Culture Initiative," Engler, Henry, Thomson Reuters, May 16, 2018.
9. https://www.societegenerale.com/en/about-us/responsibility/culture-conduct.
10. See: http://group30.org/publications/detail/166.
11. See Stephen Scott in "Bank Culture Reform: Big Banks Gain More Understanding of Staff Conduct, Lack Common Standards," Henry Engler, *Reuters*, April 24, 2018.

6

Behavioral Science: From Theory to Practice

The notion that human beings always act in their own self-interest lies at the core of modern economic theory. In recent years, that assumption has been turned on its head by pioneering economists and psychologists who have taken a closer look at how people actually behave, and incorporated their observations into what we now widely call behavioral economics and science. The early explorers in the field are Daniel Kahneman and Amos Tversky, whose collaboration led to work that revolutionized our thinking about how individuals make decisions.[1] Rather than the utility-maximizing agent that lies at the core of economic thinking, Kahneman and Tversky showed that we don't always act or behave rationally. In their seminal 1979 paper, they unveiled a concept called "prospect theory," which holds that people tend to value gains and losses differently from one another. Prospect theory suggests that losses hit us harder emotionally. For example, we are likely to feel a greater sense of loss, or emotional pain, when losing a $20 bill on the street, than joy, or happiness in finding the same bill around the corner. This finding led the economists to construct a "loss aversion" curve, which simply illustrates that most individuals are more prone to behave in a way that avoids losses than taking risks to achieve gains. Of course, there are exceptions, but the insights of Tversky and Kahneman formed the basis of what we now call behavioral economics. Their work has helped explain many of the so-called irrational decisions of humans when confronted with real-world choices. As an example, we all know people who refuse to work overtime because they believe the benefit of the extra income they would earn is outweighed by the pain of having to pay more in taxes for that additional income. Their research also helps to understand individual investing habits. For example, there is ample evidence that shows investors tend to hold on to losing stocks much longer than they hold on to winning stocks. Why? When you have a loss-making investment there is a tendency to believe that the market will turn around eventually and eradicate your losses. (Recall the description that Alexis Stenfors provided for why he held on to his enormous losses in hope of a market reversal, which in the end never arrived.) It's painful to hold stocks that are losing money, but you hold on perhaps longer than you should because of the expectation of a turnaround. Alternatively, if you have a profitable stock you're not likely to hold on to it for a long-period for fear that it will turn down in value—the "loss aversion" that is embedded in many individuals.

Kahneman later went on to build upon prospect theory and in 2011 published *Thinking, Fast and Slow*.[2] The primary thesis of the book is a dichotomy between two modes of thought: "System 1" which is fast, instinctive, emotional, almost automatic, and "System 2," a slower, more deliberative, logical and reflective mode. For example, System 1 operates when we are engaged in relatively effortless activities: driving a car; doing simple math calculations; reacting to another person's anger or threats. In other words, our reactions are almost instantaneous, with little thought or effort involved. System 2 takes over when there is a need to slow down, to be more deliberate, like filing our taxes, or signing a mortgage application. We tend to slow down and become more deliberate when using System 2.

As Haugh points out, behavioral ethics researchers have found that System 2 acts as a monitor that controls our self-interest impulses.[3] However, this monitoring function seems most effective when our cognitive load is low and more able to fully evaluate the ethical consequences of a decision. Alternatively, when cognitive load is high, the automatic system will tend to override the reflective, increasing the chance we act less ethically.

When considering the operating environment of a trading room on Wall Street, how would one categorize it based on the System 1 and 2 classifications? With multiple screens flashing, phones ringing, traders yelling across desks to other traders, salespeople screaming across to traders for a quote while a customer is on hold, rapid math calculations taking place, all in the space of seconds, this is no doubt a place where one's cognitive load is high—very high. In turn, the automatic part of the brain is in full throttle, with the reflective side barely managing a pulse. Can this help us understand the decision-making process by individuals in such high-octane work environments? One would hope the answer is yes, and that when considering large organizations we begin to identify business areas operating with high and low cognitive loads. It might well be that in complex financial organizations we will find a mix cognitive load measures given the diversity of business environments. This understanding might help tailor how we communicate with, understand, and evaluate employees in each environment. Ideally, we might develop "nudges" specifically for each environment, taking account of the differences in the cognitive load levels that employees are operating under. The nudges might be subtle, or more overt, depending on the ability of employees to use their reflective versus automatic internal processors.[4]

Behavioral Science & Banks: "The Dutch Way"

Within financial services, the Dutch National Bank (DNB) has been at the forefront of applying behavioral science, specifically in its bank supervisory process. As it explains:

> Traditionally, DNB's supervisory activities concentrated on verifying whether institutions meet the statutory requirements in terms of solvency, liquidity and controlled business operations related to solvency- and liquidity-supervision. After the crisis, this focus has broadened and deepened to a more qualitative assessment of the institution, focusing on integrity, suitability, behavior and culture of board members, in a forward looking nature, aimed at preventing problems from happening, rather than having to respond to them.[5]

The primary architects of this shift in bank supervision were Jakob de Haan and Wijnand Nuijts, who in 2013 developed the bank's "Supervisory Vision 2014-2018" strategy, which embedded the importance of looking at organizational behavior and culture in assessing the banks the DNB oversees. "By supervising cultural and behavioral patterns, DNB gains more insight into so-called root causes of risks within an organization. This enables DNB to address these root causes and thereby mitigate the risks instead of intervening in each incident and only providing 'symptom relief.'"[6]

In terms of how the bank defines culture, and its approach toward analyzing behavior at banks, the DNB relied heavily on work done by the American scholar Edgar Schein, whose classic definition of culture is: "A pattern of shared basic assumptions that the group learned as it solved problems of external adaptation and internal integration, and that have worked well enough to be considered valid and, therefore, to be taught to new members as the correct way you perceive, think, and feel in relation to those problems."[7] DNB researchers further refined their working model of organizational culture into three layers, which again was based on the work of Schein and others. The model, or "iceberg," as DNB likes to describe, has three layers: (1) behavior, which is visible in an organization (or the part of the iceberg that rests above the water); (2) group dynamics (which is just below the surface); and (3) mindset (which rests even further below). Both group dynamics and mindset are only indirectly observable within an organization, and which need to be better understood if one wants to get at the root causes of behavior. In addition to their model, the Dutch central bank has five basic assumptions that are at the root of its supervision of behavior and culture:

- Behavior and culture are ultimately the responsibility of financial institutions.
- Supervisors can identify, assess, and mitigate risks concerning behavior and culture in financial institutions.
- Behavior and culture are an integral part of the bigger organizational picture and should therefore be supervised in line with the strategy and business model, strategic organizational business goals and governance.
- Behavior and culture supervision is most effective when supervisors adopt a tailored focus in setting their expectations of financial institutions instead of "blueprinting" the right organizational culture.
- Boards of financial institutions and their top leaders are the main focus of supervision of behavior and culture.

It is perhaps worth stopping for a moment to examine at least two of the five assumptions outlined by DNB. First, there is the assumption that bank supervisors "can identify, assess and mitigate risks concerning behavior and culture" in the organizations they oversee. That is quite a powerful assumption, and one that as we have seen appears well beyond what U.S. regulators have been willing to assert, much less even contemplate in their own supervisory process. The DNB's approach toward supervision is in practice far more intrusive than that employed by U.S. regulators:

> In its supervision of behaviour and culture, DNB has a range of instruments at its disposal. For instance, it holds surveys among staff from all organisational levels, obtaining responses that should shed light on the institutions. Information is also collected by means of desk research, with an emphasis on obtaining objective information about the structure and design of the organisation and its decision-making processes. In addition, periodic interviews are

held with members of the executive board, supervisory board, and other tiers of management. These interviews focus on the interviewees' own behaviour and their perception of the dynamics within the executive or supervisory board, specifically addressing the individuals' role in the decision-making processes as well as their personal motivation and beliefs. The term 'interview' is applied loosely here – most involve an executive or supervisory director independently completing a self-assessment. Lastly, board meetings are attended on a regular basis to gain insight into the board's dynamics and behavioural patterns.[8]

During its assessment of individual banks, the DNB can uncover behaviors, particularly among senior management and boards, that are not representative of sound cultures. For example, in past examinations the bank has found "that decision-making processes are not always balanced. Dominant leadership was observed at many of the supervised institutions. In this leadership style, the leader usually uses his or her formal position or knowledge edge to force through preferred proposals in decision-making, ignoring the input of others – if at all solicited or volunteered. This jeopardises the quality of decision-making. Another risk associated with dominant leaders is that they tend to surround themselves with managers and staff that conform to their own image."[9]

Dominant leadership can lead to an environment where there is a lack of challenge in the decision-making process, a risk not only at the highest levels of the organization, but as we have seen problematic at lower levels and in mid-tier business units that are client facing. As DNB has observed, when there is a lack of challenge at the top of the organization, there will be a tendency to "to reinforce unanimity regarding the direction of the company. Although this may be beneficial insofar as it supports decisive and concerted action in the short term, it can – under certain circumstances – also foster 'groupthink'. The phenomenon of groupthink – in which the desire for consensus paves the way to premature solutions – also causes key information or risks to be overlooked. This is why dominant leadership requires opposition. Leaders who do not seek or receive feedback and who are not open to feedback will ultimately go off the rails. It is therefore important that organisations have formal systems in place for providing feedback, but often they do not."[10]

The second assumption by the DNB worth highlighting is that supervision is most effective when "supervisors adopt a tailored focus in setting their expectations of financial institutions instead of 'blueprinting' the right organizational culture." This is a critical assumption and one that resonates with what we have heard from other regulators, both in the United States and the UK. Where the DNB has gone further, however, is in its use of the supervisory process to uncover behavior among the senior leadership that can prove detrimental to a bank's *future* outcomes. This is beyond the normal practice of U.S. regulators, which tends to come into play only in circumstances where problems have already been discovered, and when the response by senior executives and board members in addressing those problems has been found lacking. The Federal Reserve's actions regarding Wells Fargo's senior management and board is a perfect example, where frustration over their ability to solve governance issues led to a "cease and desist" order. The difference in approach among regulators is noteworthy. In the DNB's case, the supervisory strategy is *preventative*, seeking to identify and mitigate behavior that can lead to problems down the road.

As we will see, there might ways in which U.S. regulators can modify their existing supervisory approach toward large institutions, short of adopting the DNB's framework. But first, we will examine how one financial institution has incorporated behavioral science tools in its own internal supervisory process.

Case Study: Royal Bank of Scotland[11]

The Royal Bank of Scotland (RBS) is one of the largest banks in the United Kingdom, with operations in the USA, Europe, and Asia. In terms of institutional size, the bank ranks 29th globally, with total assets just under $1.0 trillion.[12] The bank has a long history and most recently completed a complex restructuring to "ring-fence" its retail bank from investment bank operations, marking a major milestone in its post-financial crisis reorganization.

In 2015, RBS UK formed a Behavioral Risk team that operates within the RBS Group's Internal Audit function. The team was largely formed through the efforts of the Chief Audit Executive who believed that to better understand employee behaviors and mitigate potential risk, the audit function needed expertise in organizational psychology and behavioral science. Currently, the Behavioral Risk team has five members and is led by Wieke Scholten, a former supervisor of behavior and culture at the Dutch National Bank. To date, the team has completed 15 "deep-dive" reviews in areas of the bank that include approximately 100–500 employees on average. In July 2018, Scholten, along with senior manager, Shweta Pajpani, discussed the role and structure of the team, its methodology for conducting reviews, and how its findings are used in the organization.

Formation of the Team in 2015

The behavioral risk team was created in 2015 under the direction of the bank's Chief Audit Executive. At the time, a consultant specializing in organizational psychology was working within Internal Audit, and together with the Chief Auditor and the Chief Audit Executive, helped to lay the foundations of the small group. During this period, there was also guidance published by the UK's Chartered Institute of Internal Audit that focused on Internal Audit's role in assessing culture, adding to the team's thinking and initial development. However, the critical factor has been the direction from the Chief Audit Executive and his experience in seeing cultural and behavioral causes lying behind many of the issues banks had encountered. Internal Audit worked intensively with HR and Risk while establishing the Behavioral Risk work and team, given the important roles both functions have in driving the bank-wide organizational and risk cultural direction.

"I think the key distinguishing factor within all of this is the direction we got and continue to get from our Chief Auditor and Chief Audit Executive. They have been able to acknowledge that in order to assess behaviors a foundation in organizational psychology or behavioral science or the equivalent is fundamental," said Shweta Pajpani.

The larger context for such a unit has also been the financial crisis, and many of the issues arising from that period. As with many large financial firms, RBS had its share of problems. The bank has been involved in high-profile scandals, including the Libor manipulation case and collusion in foreign exchange markets.

"Ultimately, we needed to ensure that our work from a preventative perspective can help avoid future issues. It's about regaining that trust," said Pajpani.

Behavioral Risk: How to Measure?

Bankers are quite numbers driven, and being able to measure risk is a critical aspect of the business. Whether the risk is credit-related, operational, or focuses on liquidity or interest rates, the ability to measure is paramount. However, when it comes to less tangible concepts such as behavior or culture there has been a tendency by many within the financial community to struggle over how to incorporate them within the existing risk framework. How does one measure cultural fitness, for example? Can one really observe and analyze employee behavior in a meaningful way? Is it possible to quantify and identify whether progress is being made to improve behavior and mitigate potential risks?

For the RBS team this was part of the initial challenge. By using a combination of quantitative and qualitative factors, the team has been able to demonstrate that behavioral risk can be measured in much the same way as other risks.

"We are trying to identify behavioral risk as a standalone risk that you need to assess, manage, and mitigate, just as you would credit risk, for example," said Wieke Scholten. Importantly, while much of the internal and external environment in which banks operate can be quantified, what managers do with that information is what counts at the end of the day, and in Scholten's view, there is a "qualitative" aspect to any financial risk metric.

"I would argue that any other risk, even though they are seemingly easier to quantify, you still need some qualitative observations and professional judgment to assess that risk," Scholten said. "It's not just that here's a number and hence you know the truth. That number still needs to be assessed and judged with professional expertise, the same as if you use data from a behavioral risk review."

Review Selection Process

As noted, the team engages in "deep dive" reviews of areas within the bank that warrant attention, typically groups that average between 100 and 500 employees. An important factor behind limiting the size of the group to around 500 is to provide in-depth and granular insights that are specific to a certain "sub-culture" and allow management to translate these insights into action. How the areas are selected is critical and reliant upon the input of both internal and external stakeholders. There are essentially four primary inputs to the selection process. As the Behavioral Risk team is part of Group Internal Audit, the initial inputs to the selection process come from auditors assigned to various lines of business across the organization.

The team has developed an approach for auditors which includes templates designed to capture certain forms of behavior. As Pajpani describes, having auditors assist the team this way is an additional task for them and required training to bring them up to speed on what they should be looking for.

"We designed templates that are prescriptive enough but also open enough to capture the qualitative richness of what they're seeing," said Pajpani. Some of the specific behaviors that auditors capture in their reports include leadership, decision-making, group dynamics, and communication. In addition, there are more risk-focused categories in line with RBS' Risk

Culture framework, such as transparency, acknowledgment, responsiveness, and respect.

These observations are pulled together each quarter for the team. The objective of the findings is to identify what some of the "hot spots" might be within certain business units and the undesirable behaviors that are observed by the auditors.

A second input are the views of the chief audit executive and his leadership team—audit executives who are responsible for individual business lines. The team has conversations with each executive to understand what they are seeing in terms of potential hot spots. Given that they operate at a higher level within the bank they might be seeing behaviors that are not captured on the ground by auditors. Their observations are collected and fed into the review process.

External stakeholders within the bank—human resources, risk (which includes compliance), and legal—are the third input to the process. Given their position within the bank as the so-called second line of defense, they bring perspectives that might be different from those within the audit function. While the team meets with these groups throughout the year, once a year the team will meet with them, typically around the third quarter, to specifically discuss their views to help develop the behavioral risk team's plan for the following year.

"We often ask them the question: 'If you were us, where would you go?'" said Pajpani. "They have hots spots in mind from their own interactions, bank-wide dashboards and measurement reports, and these insights are valuable for us to consider."

At times, those insights might be across the organization, capturing behaviors that are occurring in more than one business unit.

Lastly, there is data, primarily in the form of "management information" metrics and other indicators (key performance indicators, for example) that are captured by units such as compliance, and included in the overall assessment of which areas the team should investigate.

"We look at HR data, such as absenteeism and turnover, for example. We also examine more grievance, investigative-type of data, where we try to understand what the current landscape is in terms of investigations," said Scholten. Some of this data can include "whistleblower" investigations, for example.

Management information data is useful in the process, said Scholten, but one needs to be cautious in what the data is telling you. From a management perspective, there might be a tendency to say: "I have green dashboards, so everything is fine."

"It would be better to say: 'I have green dashboards, that's good, step one. Now, I'm curious about what is happening at the working floor level' … information you wouldn't typically get through a survey," she added.

While data is an important input, the information needs to be supplemented by qualitative judgments in deciding which group to investigate. These qualitative assessments come from talking to various stakeholders across the organization, said Scholten. "The question of 'where would you go if you were us' is a very powerful question,' because often people within the bank know when 'something is happening over there.'"

"Deep Dives": How Do They Work?

There are five components to a "deep dive" review once a business group or specific area is selected by the Behavioral Risk team. They include the following:

- *Surveys*: Independently commissioned by the team, surveys include questions that go to the entire population of the group under review, and include a scale that ranges from "strongly agree" to "strongly disagree."
- *Confidential conversations*: Using a representative sample of the group, which will include different teams and jurisdictions if needed, the team holds a series of one-on-one conversations with employees. The discussions are conversational in tone, and seek to understand what types of behaviors are occurring within the group or are typical for that area. For example, understanding what behavioral patterns and aspects of the local climate are potentially driving poor outcomes.
- *Focus groups*: Somewhat larger, group conversations are held with a maximum of 10 individuals at the same level. As with the one-on-one conversations, the objective is to gain an insight into behavioral patterns and aspects of the climate specific to that area or business.
- *Formal environment*: For example, included in this review might be leadership communications, governance structures, and how performance is managed. Overall, what is written on paper can influence behavior so this element is examined to gain a better understanding.
- *Independent observations*: The final component includes team members attending leadership or staff meetings, or observing working floor contexts to gain a perspective on, for instance, group dynamics and interactions.

After the information from all five components are collected, the team analyzes the data, looking for common patterns and themes. These behavioral observations need to be as specific as possible so that there are actions the business group can take to mitigate the perceived risks.

The outcomes or findings vary and can be, but are not always, about misconduct, said Scholten. "It could also be about poor decision-making, or poor management of risk in general," she said. "It could be driving executional risk or operational or strategic risk."

"Our output is area or business specific, because that is how we can make it actionable and effective in terms of mitigating the behavioral risk in that area," Scholten added. "But having done 15 reviews so far, at some point you can also identify behaviors occurring group-wide that you might want to improve."

Dissemination of Findings

Once the findings are complete, the team develops a detailed report that is initially discussed with the executive in charge of the business unit, usually at the CEO minus two, or three level. (For example: the senior managing director in charge of a certain business.) After a few weeks, the report is discussed more broadly with the executive's management committee—the executive's direct reports—and other key stakeholders (e.g., the business' HR Partner).

After these initial meetings, an official audit finding is raised and given a specific classification, with "major" being the most severe. The finding requires the management of the group to pull together a plan of how they are going to mitigate the behavior risk identified by the team.

"We ask them to keep the particular issue open in our risk management systems for at least 18 months," said Pajpani, allowing sufficient time for each group to come up with a mitigation plan. Some issues can be addressed more quickly than others, but given the nature of the subject matter, it typically requires more time for management teams to address the drivers identified.

While the primary purpose of the findings is to identify behavioral risk within a business area that needs to be mitigated, a second objective is to increase awareness higher up the managerial chain, including board level members, said Scholten. And as the review process increases in number, themes emerge group-wide that allow the team to create specific reports for board-level committees.

Reactions from the Business

As with any internal audit function, the business under the lens will not necessarily greet the findings with open arms. Under certain scenarios, the team's report may include behaviors of teams who are high-revenue producers, for example. How does the team deal with situations where the business heads are reluctant to change?

"I think our general observation is that stakeholders sometimes have trouble with accepting what we reveal initially… but often recognize the value of our observations in a second instance …," said Scholten. The findings of the team are disseminated among various risk committees.

"We always give management the time to go away and do what they said they were going to do. But we make it quite clear that we are going to come back and follow up," added Pajpani. "We look to see whether there has been enough of a shift to identify whether the group is moving in the right direction."

"We've definitely seen that our work has had an effect and impact, and that they have taken the observations we made on-board and tried to come up with ways to initiate behavioral change. Some areas have limited experience in impacting behaviours so it isn't always easy for them," she added.

Part of the difficulty for some business heads is that they may lack the required specific skills to address complex behavioral issues. When added to the list of existing demands and pressures they are under, fixing behavioral risks among their staff is not something they are normally accustomed to or necessarily equipped to do.

"It's not easy to improve your local climate at the side of your desk without having specific expertise and skills in cultural change," noted Scholten.

Which leads to a critical factor for any behavioral risk team in an Internal Audit position: is it positioned properly within the organization to impact adverse local climates?

Independent Role Is Critical

How a behavioral risk team is positioned within an organization will very much determine its effectiveness. Most important, such a unit needs to have independence from other functions, along with the requisite support and buy-in from senior management.

"You need independence to make your own selection, or we would not be able to go to those high-risk areas," said Scholten.

Additionally, while the team should work toward "actionable" findings, it cannot be seen playing a consultative or advisory role to the business group under review. In other words, it can't tell the business unit how to fix the problem it has identified and is required to follow-up on. In that sense, the organization needs to support management to provide the resources and training to address the issues found by the team.

"We should be as clear and proactive as we can be without prescribing what businesses should do to mitigate behavioural risk," said Scholten. "But we also need to be as supportive as we can in that stage where management designs an approach to address the problem."

Behavioral Risk Team: Right Mix of Skills

The RBS behavioral risk team is currently the only one of its kind among large UK banks. The team of five has a mix of experience: some are organizational or social psychologists while others come from finance, audit, or risk backgrounds. How to obtain the right skills sets is by no means easy. Ideal candidates would have psychological expertise as well as a deep understanding of how large financial institutions work.

"When you look at the makeup of our team some do have a psychology background and there are some who have experience of doing behavioural risk reviews. The impact is in the balance," said Pajpani, who herself came from an audit and consultancy background, and is now pursuing advanced studies in psychology.

But according to Scholten, some of the psychological skills can also be acquired on the job. Her own experience is instructive, having joined the DNB as an organizational psychologist, yet going on to become a bank supervisor, conducting formal reviews of numerous banks in the Netherlands and Europe before coming to RBS.

"I would never say only academic psychologists can do this work. You can acquire enough knowledge about risks of behaviours in a professional context without doing a PhD in psychology," she said. However, using psychological theory as a basis for the methodology used has been one of the success factors of this work.

Noteworthy Observations

In reviewing the practices of the Behavioral Risk team at RBS in London, there are several points worth highlighting, which might prove beneficial to any institution contemplating a similar approach. First, the behavioral risk team is structured within the organization as a critical supplement to existing core functions (e.g., compliance, human resources, risk). These existing functions have their own duties and responsibilities, but in carrying out their job they inevitably are *observers* of behavior. If we use the DNB "iceberg" model of behavior and culture, these control functions see what is occurring above the water line, so to speak. They interact with staff and personnel of various business units on a regular basis and over time can identify, sense, intuit behaviors that might be risky in nature. The question posed by the RBS team—"Where would you go?"—when determining which areas of the bank require a "deep dive" is a very powerful one, for it recognizes that there is existing organizational or institutional knowledge concerning behavior that might require intervention. In other words, there is intelligence that is readily available about potential "blind spots" within the organization—it just needs to be captured, collected and analyzed. That role or activity is not one that is currently an explicit responsibility for any of the aforementioned functions. While compliance may be viewed as the "cop on the beat," its primary role is to assist business units in *complying* with existing rules and regulations, both internal and externally-driven. One can argue that it should also escalate to senior management behavior that it believes puts the firm at risk, but as we have often seen and heard, compliance staff tend to view themselves on the weaker end of the relationship they have with business heads. Which leads to a second observation: independence. As Scholten and Pajpani emphasized, it is critical that their group has independence from other functions and businesses, and allowed to roam the organization for problem areas. This role and responsibility is made explicit, so that the rest of organization understands their purpose. This explicit mandate is what gives value to role they play as guardians of the institution; as gatherers of intelligence, and a "second pair of eyes" on behaviors that put the firm at risk.

Uncovering Good and Bad Behavior

While the focus of the RBS team is on uncovering undesirable behaviors, one can easily see how the process might also lead one to areas where there are not such risks; groups where employees are exhibiting the types of behavior one would like to see replicated across the entire firm. As we all know, there are behavioral issues within most large institutions bubbling beneath the surface, often masked by exceptional business performance and results, or complacency by those in charge. At the same time, there are pockets or business units that are both performing and behaving well. Any behavioral risk team within a financial services firm will come to understand who is behaving well while also delivering on the goals and objectives of management. Let's call these groups "non-hot spots" for the moment, a metric that can be collected and analyzed by the behavioral risk team over the course of its organizational-wide assessment process. As the team gathers its intelligence, it can document the characteristics and behaviors that would appear to be working well. For example, what is the decision-making process like? Are senior business executives open to challenge by their employees? If they are, how is that working out in practice? What are the methods and means of communication by the heads of these groups that are seen effective? Are they doing things outside the norms of the organization? In other words, what are the identifiable behaviors of successful groups that we can document and perhaps learn from? In collecting such information, can we apply what we have learned to other areas, be it in terms of behavioral styles or techniques, or incentives for employees that are not seen elsewhere in the organization? While the initial role and responsibilities of a behavioral risk are to identify behaviors that pose risks, such a team could also benefit the organization as custodian of behaviors and management styles that are proving effective. In other words, there can be two processes or parts to the role of such group, as outlined below (Fig. 6.1).

In the team's primary function, they can be seen as a "risk mitigator." But they can also serve to develop techniques—perhaps "nudges"—that arise over the course of their research, interactions with businesses and other support functions, and senior management. By combining both efforts, such a team might become a "choice architect" and thereby help management develop what Thaler and Sunstein have called a "choice architecture" for the organizations, one that emphasizes the shared-purpose and cultural norms that may be articulated by senior management, but in practice are difficult to achieve.

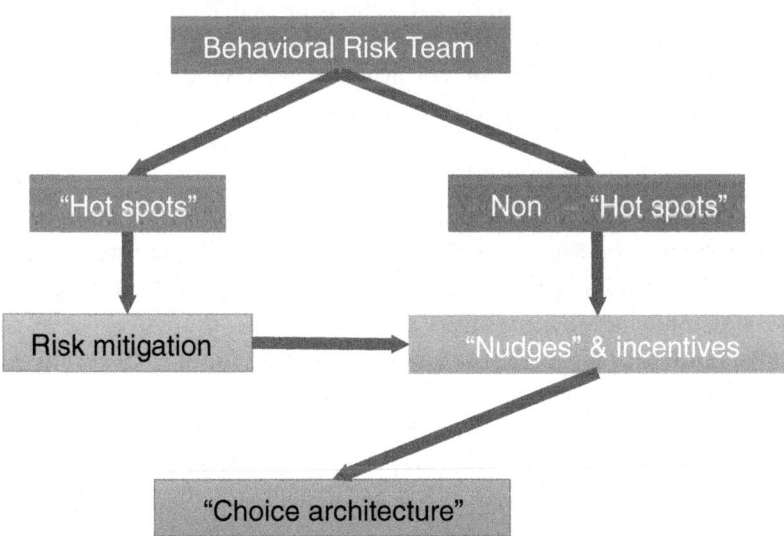

Fig. 6.1 Path toward a "choice architecture"

Choice Architecture: Initial Thoughts

Choice architecture simply reflects the fact that there are many ways to present a choice to those making decisions. How one makes a decision, or choice, often depends on how the choice is presented. Those in charge of designing the architecture or presentation of choices—the architects—have an important and influential role to play. Sometimes by varying the presentation of choices, one can influence which choices or decisions are made. In much of the literature on choice architecture so far, the focus of applying behavioral science has been in areas where there is a broad economic imperative, such as increasing personal savings. For example, programs have been implemented where employees commit in advance to allocating a portion of their future salary increases toward retirement savings. The results have shown that a high percentage (78%) of those offered the plan joined, and that the majority of those enrolled in the plan (80%) remained in it through a fourth pay raise. Moreover, the average saving rates for those in the program increased from 3.5% to 13.6% over the course of 40 months.[13]

What you are trying to do as a choice architect is "nudge" behavior in a certain direction without making the decision maker feel or believe that they have no options in the decision process. Or as Thaler and Sunstein put it, a nudge is:

> … any aspect of the choice architecture that alters people's behavior in a predictable way without forbidding any options or significantly changing their economic incentives. To count as a mere nudge, the intervention must be easy and cheap to avoid. Nudges are not mandates. Putting the fruit at eye level counts as a nudge. Banning junk food does not.[14]

It would seem that "nudging" is a lot about aligning or architecting incentives to modify behavior in a direction that is beneficial to the individual or group, but at the same time doesn't feel imposed, or constricting. How such nudging is used within a corporate environment will ultimately have to do with how various incentives are presented to the employee or manager. We have previously discussed how the partnership model during earlier times on Wall Street appeared to nudge behavior toward keeping a closer eye on what was going on in the firm. The incentives were in the form of huge personal and financial loss if one didn't keep things in check—"loss aversion" at its most extreme. How incentives might be aligned within today's financial organizations that both encourage ethical behavior while also delivering stated financial goals and objectives could be part of the mission of behavioral risk teams. As they uncover what works and doesn't work in their organizations they will be able to identify tools—nudges—that can be applied in areas where they wish to encourage better behavior, and ultimately build strong cultures. It is an area that is worth further research and understanding.

Notes

1. Kahneman, Daniel, and Tversky, Amos. (1979). "Prospect Theory: An Analysis of Decision Under Risk," *Econometrica*, Vol. 47, No. 2 (March), pp. 263–292.
2. *Thinking, Fast and Slow*, Daniel Kahneman, Farrar, Straus and Giroux, 2011.
3. Haugh, Todd. (2017). "Nudging Corporate Compliance," *American Business Law Journal*, Vol. 54, Issue 4, pp. 683–741, Winter 2017.
4. "Nudges" is a behavioral science term developed by Richard Thaler and Cass Sunstein to describe how positive reinforcement and indirect suggestions or methods can be used to influence the behavior of individuals and groups.
5. "Supervision of Behavior and Culture—Foundations, Practice & Future Developments," De Nederlandsche Bank, 2015.
6. Ibid.
7. Schein, E. H. (1984). "Coming to a New Awareness of Organizational Culture," *Sloan Management Review*, Vol. 25, Issue 2, pp. 3–16.
8. "Supervising Culture and Behaviour at Financial Institutions: The Experience of De Nederlandsche Bank," Jakob de Haan, Wijnand Nuijts, and Mirea Raaijmakers, VOX CEPR Policy Portal, *VOX CEPR Policy Portal*, November 2015.
9. Ibid.
10. Ibid.
11. Based on interview with Wieke Scholten & Shweta Pajpani, Royal Bank of Scotland, London, UK, July 2018.
12. S&P Global Market Intelligence (2018).
13. Thaler, Richard, and Benartzi, Shlomo. (2004). "Save More Tomorrow™: Using Behavioral Economics to Increase Employee Saving," *Journal of Political Economy* (February).
14. *Nudge—Improving Decisions About Health, Wealth and Happiness*, Richard Thaler, Cass Sunstein, Penguin Books, 2009.

7

U.S. Regulators: Requiring Behavioral Risk Teams

We have seen how behavioral science, defined in the broad sense of the term, can be applied within large financial firms to identify behaviors that pose risks to the organization. At RBS the approach is proactive, designed to uncover blind spots well before a much larger problem emerges. The strategy leverages the knowledge, insights, and expertise of individuals trained in psychology, group dynamics, and other social sciences. But more importantly, the behavioral risk team exists because certain individuals within the organization recognized that one can't rely solely on existing functions—compliance, human resources, audit, risk management—to understand employee behavior. They also recognize that for cultural change to be effective, one needs to go beyond establishing "culture programs" and other one-time initiatives that hope to bring about lasting and effective change.

We also find that the behavioral risk team is led by a former bank supervisor—in this case, one who previously worked at the Dutch National Bank, an innovative outlier among regulators in its approach toward bank supervision. The evidence at RBS would tend to suggest there is value in integrating such a team within the existing framework of a bank's other functions. The value comes not only from the team itself and its unique perspective, but also from coordinating and leveraging the existing knowledge base, insights and untapped perspectives from other functions. In other words, it appears that such a team can fill an existing gap within the organization when it comes to understanding employee behavior and the risks involved. The information is already available within the organization. It just needs someone to organize, collect, analyze, and disseminate the intelligence. This role is different and unique, and one that most organizations lack.

If this perspective is accurate, it seems fair to ask why other institutions are not following suit? Perhaps they are and we're simply unaware of their plans and strategies. (To this writer's knowledge, there is another large European bank that is in the early stages of building a behavioral risk team.) But also likely is that there is growing complacency at many organizations, having come off a decade of absorbing regulatory mandates that have put them on a stronger financial footing. Higher capital levels, increased regulatory reporting, limits on the scope and type of businesses they can engage in, all have contributed to a view that we are in better shape today than before the crisis. This perspective is also reflected in rising share prices and a sense of well-being that tempers the need for additional efforts to mitigate risk—whether employee-related or otherwise. Some senior executives, however, would argue that it is exactly during such good times that one needs to remain vigilant; that risks might be lurking within your organization that aren't visible due to superb performance. "It really helps to be a little paranoid and a little scarred …Forget about what the regulators want, what the public want, what the politicians want; we don't want [another crisis]," said James Gorman, chief executive of Morgan Stanley in June 2018.[1]

While trying to discern the prevailing sentiment across the industry may prove difficult, it's clear that the leadership of many U.S. institutions have the view that the regulations put in place after the crisis have been onerous, complex, and costly. There is a need to tailor, fine-tune or recalibrate existing rules, they argue, and apparently their voice has been heard. The Federal Reserve and other U.S. regulators have put forward proposals to amend certain rules and in other instances less apt to enforce existing rules with the same rigor as before. The shift reflects the prevailing view of the Trump administration, which through the U.S. Treasury has adopted a more business-friendly approach toward financial regulation. In such a climate, it's difficult to see U.S. institutions lining up to create behavioral risk teams without being required to do so. The dominant attitude today is likely to be "we've done quite a bit on the conduct and culture front and believe it's sufficient for now." Indeed, U.S. regulators have applauded the efforts by banks to address such issues and noted that the organizations they oversee are now much more cognizant of the importance of monitoring behavior. In such a context, it is unlikely that U.S. banks will follow the lead of RBS.

Bank Supervision: Facilitate or Lead?

U.S. bank regulators have made explicit the limitations they face when it comes to conduct and culture issues: they are not willing to prescribe what banks should do because they are not equipped to do so. Moreover, adopting a rules-based approach would be counterproductive, allowing banks to treat such issues in much the same way they would other forms of regulation. What regulators can do—and this has been demonstrated most clearly by the Federal Reserve Bank of New York—is through its convening powers bring together stakeholders across the industry to discuss and debate how best to tackle such difficult issues as well as monitor progress. To this end, the efforts by the New York Fed to facilitate this dialogue, which is now in its sixth year, has been highly effective and well-received by the community, both here and abroad. But after a multitude of conversations, conferences, white papers and speeches, have we learned anything that can be put into practice? In other words, can U.S. regulators take steps on the culture front that more explicitly require banks to act in certain ways, short of prescribing a set of rules? It would appear they can, and at this point, should. The risks of not doing so are considerable, particularly as institutional memories of the financial crisis fade.

What specifically should U.S. regulators do? They should require large, complex institutions they oversee to include behavioral risk units in their organizations. As a first step, U.S. banking organizations that qualify as global systemically important banks (G-SIBs) should fall under this requirement. According to the Financial Stability Board, at the end of 2017 there were eight U.S. institutions that were deemed G-SIBs: JPMorgan Chase, Bank of America, Citigroup, Goldman Sachs, Wells Fargo, Bank of New York Mellon, Morgan Stanley and State Street. All of these institutions would benefit from having an independent behavioral risk function that would supplement the work of its compliance, audit, human resources, legal and risk management groups. The costs of establishing these teams would be minimal in comparison to the value and benefits derived from the identification and analysis of behavioral trouble spots in their organizations. How these units are structured should be left up to them, with the critical factor being their independence from other functions and businesses. Ideally, such teams would have a direct reporting line into the chief executive officer of the institution. Leadership and direction at the very top would send an unequivocal message to managers and employees of the importance of this new unit, and how the management of conduct, behavior and cultural issues is a continuous effort, not something that one does only in response to a crisis. Alternatively, as we have seen at RBS, the team could report up to the chief audit executive, or possibly to the chief risk officer. Again, the critical feature is independence. Without this it means little where the unit would sit within the organization.

Which U.S. regulator should take the lead with these organizations? Given the work the Federal Reserve Bank of New York has done and expertise developed, the requirement should come from the Board of Governors of the Federal Reserve System. The proposal for the rule should be based on a range of inputs from experts in the field, including other regulators and central banks who have had experience in applying behavioral science in their supervisory functions. The Dutch National Bank would be an obvious candidate along with the UK's Financial Conduct Authority. Indeed, such collaboration has already been seen with the work DNB has done with the Central Bank of Ireland.[2] In July 2018, Ireland's central bank published a report, detailing the findings of the collaboration with the DNB. The focus of the reviews, which included its five main retail banks—AIB Group, Bank of Ireland Group, permanent tsb, Ulster Bank Ireland, and KBC Bank Ireland—was primarily "on the behavior of executive leadership teams of each bank as well as the interplay of senior executives and internal stakeholders in the context of strategic decision-making. As such, they represent a snapshot at a point in time with a particular focus on the key decision-makers in each firm who set the tone from the top," the central bank said. Among the review's findings, two important prerequisites for successful transformation were not met in all instances. These are:

- A collective understanding of what consumer focus means and what behavior it requires.
- An embedded consumer focus in structures, processes and systems.

The report also highlighted the following issues that may jeopardize the successful transformation toward a consumer-focused culture:

- Several executive committees display "firefighting behavior," focusing on urgent and short-term issues, thereby hampering their capacity to design a long-term cultural transformation process.
- Some banks continue to display remnants of the crisis-era mindset resulting in occasional reversal to directive, or "command and control," leadership styles when the emphasis should be on collaborative approaches.
- There is a need to increase empowerment and decision-making ability of senior staff, in order to decrease executives' decision burden and enable the organization to execute the transformation.

- The reviews also found concerns around overoptimism regarding the successful transition to a consumer-focused culture.
- The Diversity and Inclusion Assessments reveal banks have more work to do to ensure their organizations are sufficiently diverse and inclusive.

Commenting on the findings of the report, Derville Rowland, Director General Financial Conduct, said: "Culture is set from the top down. It is a matter for boards and senior management, in the first instance, to set an effective culture that places the best interests of their customers first. Banks still have a distance to go to live up to their slogans of putting customers first." To address the perceived shortcomings, the central bank required each bank "to devise action plans in response to the institution-specific findings of the Behaviour and Culture Reviews. Supervisors will assess the actions planned by the banks and engage on progress being made." The central bank also proposed the introduction of a new "Individual Accountability Framework" which would apply to banks and other regulated financial service providers. The framework includes conduct standards for regulated financial services providers and the staff working in them, a "Senior Executive Accountability Regime," as well enhancements to the existing "Fitness & Probity Regime" and enforcement process.

While the collaboration between the Central Bank of Ireland and the DNB did not go so far as requiring each of the five leading retail banks to establish behavioral risk teams, the focus of its findings clearly emphasized the need for greater attention to conduct and behavior.

In the United States, the New York Fed could play a consultative role with the banks required to form such teams, leveraging its knowledge, expertise, and convening powers with other banks, regulators, and those in the academic community who could provide guidance and insight. Given that many of the banks affected might struggle in how to establish such teams—identifying the right skill sets and candidates, for example—the Federal Reserve could aid the process by running working groups to give each institution an opportunity to discuss how best to develop behavioral risk teams. In addition, given the unique character of such a rule, the Federal Reserve could play a collaborative role with banks in the initial stages of adoption. This would be a learning exercise for the Fed and the banks, and the knowledge and insights gained from the introduction of such teams at these institutions would have benefits for both sides. Over time, one could envision enhanced collaboration between banks, the Federal Reserve and business school programs, with the latter possibly including behavioral training and courses as part of their curriculums. (A deeper discussion of the role business schools can play on culture, ethics and behavior will be included in the next section.)

What would be the likely response to such a requirement? One possible criticism would be in how one would assess the value of behavioral risk teams. Specifically, how would you measure progress? The question is fair enough, but also difficult to answer given the subject matter. How would you know whether your early intervention in a certain business unit of your organization stopped a larger problem for developing? There is no simple retrospective technique or tool that can provide the answer, much less a quantifiable one. However, this difficulty should not be a justifiable impediment. After all, why do we have various risk management functions across the institution? Is it possible to do a post-event calculation on the losses avoided by having sound credit risk systems in place during an economic and financial downturn? A large bank—and smaller ones as well—have such controls in place because they are required to do so by regulators. We have come to a point where the costs of misconduct and unethical behavior have been well-documented across the industry. Implementing small-scale behavior risk teams would appear to be a cost worth absorbing, particularly when compared with the risk of much higher costs arising from misconduct that is identified too late.

Role for Business Schools

There is growing recognition that the culture battle on Wall Street is one that extends beyond the walls of its institutions. One of the uncomfortable side effects of misconduct and ethical failures has been on those attending the country's leading business schools. Deans at some of these organizations have voiced concern over how young graduates have become less attracted to the financial sector, owing in large measure to what they perceive as toxic cultures. "We've been having a number of business school deans come in and talk to us at the New York Fed over the last few years, and what they say is that there are people who will actually not go into the financial services industry because of this bad conduct. That's not a good cycle. If the most ethical people coming out of the business schools decide that they are not going to go into this industry, that means there's quite a bit more work to do," said William Dudley, president of the New York Fed, at a Reuters Breakingviews conference in February 2018.[3]

Following Dudley's remarks, the New York Fed held a conference on conduct and culture in June 2018, which included a discussion of the role that business schools can play in restoring ethics in financial services. Among the observations of the leading academics, deans of business schools, and industry executives, several stood out.

First, financial firms have moved away from rotational programs and toward specialization. We have discussed how there is increased emphasis on technical skills, for example, as the business of Wall Street becomes more wedded to technology and automation. However, this development "can make it more difficult to attract well-rounded leaders and ensure staff has an enterprise-level perspective on desired cultural norms," according to the New York Fed's conference findings. Second, staff at large financial firms turn over quickly, with a large percentage of employees today not even present at the financial crisis. Will Bousquette, a senior executive at Goldman Sachs, noted that 78% of Goldman's employees did not work there during the financial crisis. "Lessons about culture, finance, and society learned firsthand during the crisis now need to be imparted to a new generation," the bank wrote in a summary of the conference findings.[4] Third, financial firms increasingly want to hire staff that already have a strong understanding of ethical decision-making, particularly in difficult situations. With the help of universities and business schools, the hope is that their curriculums will include a "better understanding of the drivers of culture and the interplay between incentives and ethical decision-making."

After years of informal discussions between the New York Fed, banks, and universities, the regulator has launched a "standing forum" for business schools and financial firms which intends to "drive action from the partnership on cultural reform efforts." What can some of these efforts look like? Outlining their own ideas in a separate essay in 2018, Scott DeRue, dean of the Ross School of Business at Michigan University and Bousquette of Goldman Sachs, offered a few potential areas for research[5]:

- What if … we commissioned a white paper by organizational or behavioral scientists at multiple schools focused on how banks are strengthening their culture of ethics and integrity?
- What if … companies sponsored on-site talks by researchers who can demonstrate (with data) that positive business practices improve profits?
- What if … a consortium of banks and schools teamed up to develop a series of case studies on ethics in financial services?

Might such a forum consider the role that behavioral risk teams can play in financial firms, and include work done by the RBS group as well as the views of the DNB? Clearly, the answer is yes, and the hope is that such a regular gathering of business schools and industry participants invites experts from organizations that are putting theory into practice. According to senior officials at the New York Fed, the goal of such a forum—the first of which would be held in the spring of 2019—would be to have a culture ethics "challenge" sponsored by firms and business schools where competing teams would address such issues. In the long run, the view is for such the forum to become "self-sustaining," and allow firms to determine what types of graduates they are looking for. Another idea that might gather traction, say officials, is for leading behavioral and organizational psychology experts at such universities to conduct case studies within participating banks to identify cultural and behavioral lapses. It's been observed that academics often struggle to gain access to large financial firms so they can capture data for their research. Through the New York Fed forum, mutual benefit is likely to arise on both sides, with university experts providing "free consulting" services to the banks through such case studies. "I think that would be an easy sell on both sides," said one official.

Such collaboration might also become fertile ground for both sides to better understand how behavioral science might be operationalized within financial companies. As we have argued, to the extent that behavioral risk teams become part of the infrastructure at large institutions, there will be a need for individuals with the right mix of skills and expertise. Universities might find themselves adapting to such a need by incorporating specialized courses on organizational psychology into their business school curriculums. It is the hope that the New York Fed's forum leads to the type of cooperation and information sharing that brings behavioral science expertise to financial firms, whether mandated or not.

Notes

1. "Morgan Stanley's Gorman Warns Wall St to Be 'Paranoid,'" Ben McLannahan, *Financial Times*, June 18, 2018.
2. "Behavior and Culture of the Irish Retail Banks,"Central Bank of Ireland, July 2018: https://www.centralbank.ie/publication/behaviour-and-culture-report.
3. "Transcript of Banking Culture—Still Room for Improvement? Panel Discussion at Thomson Reuters, New York City, February 7, 2018," Federal Reserve Bank of New York: https://www.newyorkfed.org/newsevents/speeches/2018/dud180209.
4. https://www.newyorkfed.org/medialibrary/media/governance-and-culture-reform/2018-NewYorkFed-Culture-Conference-Summary.pdf.
5. https://medium.com/new-york-fed/reinforcing-ethics-in-financial-services-c56bf01b5ca0.

8

What Is Finance For?

There are forces at work in financial services, and the larger economy, that appear to have near unrelenting, unstoppable momentum, and for which, at least now, seem to have no visible roadblocks ahead. We have outlined one of them, which is size and concentration. U.S. financial institutions are, ten years after the crisis, larger and more powerful than before. There may be many reasons for this, with some arguing that post-crisis regulation contributed to the outcome, prompting banks to become bigger to pay for the costs of added new rules and curbs on their activities. Maybe. This is an area that is rich for further research. Whatever the cause, we are stuck with the reality. While there has been much hand-wringing over "too big to fail," our biggest banks today are, indeed, too big to go the way of Lehman Brothers in 2008. And while bankers still suffer in popularity with the American electorate, there isn't a public clamoring for breaking up the organizations they run. That sentiment is also reflected in a Congress that has endorsed a "re-balancing" of Dodd Frank rules, believing big banks have suffered long enough. Apart from Senator Elizabeth Warren's continued crusade against the mega-sized institutions, no one else seems willing to join the cause. Meanwhile, the Trump administration's agenda has been supportive of big bank regulatory relief, with size and concentration nowhere to be found as a concern in its policy pronouncements.

Another force at work is technology, and here there are two important dynamics. The first dynamic is the ongoing automation of financial markets and services, in many cases led by the largest institutions. This trend has been in place for many years, with its roots well before the 2008 upheaval. There is little doubt it will continue. Automation of financial markets, whether through the continued movement away from over-the-counter transactions, or the ongoing spread and use of algorithmic trading, is a force that is core to the business model of many firms. The benefits are in execution, speed, and most importantly, cost reduction, with fewer staff needed to execute transactions and achieve greater market share and penetration. While this dynamic is clear, and seemingly unstoppable in financial markets, the use of technology in other parts of the business—consumer banking, wholesale lending, asset management, and increasingly support functions, such as compliance and operations—continues as well.

The second dynamic concerning technology is its risks—specifically, cybersecurity and the threat of attack. Perhaps more than any other risk today, this is the one that keeps chief executives up at night. The financial industry is spending vast sums on cybersecurity, but that spend pales in comparison to the potential damage that could be inflicted, not only on one single organization, but on the banking system as whole in the event of a major attack. Countless surveys and interviews with senior executives put this at the top of their concerns. While there are growing signs of cooperation and collaboration among firms to guard against the threat, no one knows whether such efforts are enough. The problem might be analogous to a cosmic "wormhole"—no one has ever been through one, or knows if it's even possible.

A byproduct of these powerful technological forces has been the accumulation and use of data, and rising concerns over individual privacy. Large banking firms have in the past been likened to "information giants," given the critical role that data plays in moving money around the globe. That role, the information that banks have, together with the growth of the technology sector, and its own concentrated power and access to personal information, has opened the door to possible alliances between the two. The latter are clearly interested in such collaboration.[1] One can argue that the economic concentration in the technology sector—Amazon, Google, and Facebook, for example—and the increased concentration of financial services presents a set of unprecedented risks and challenges. We have already seen how data and information can be used to effect political outcomes. What other types of risks might unfold should tech and banking giants join forces is beyond the scope of this book and author's imagination. Which naturally begs the question: what does any of this have to do with conduct and culture in financial services?

The role of finance in society has always been, at a basic level, about the transfer of capital from those who have it, to those who need it. It's a critical role in the functioning of the economy, hence, the need for regulatory oversight. Bankers have long had a fiduciary responsibility to their clients and customers, to ensure that the advice provided and intermediary role they play is in the interests of those they serve. What we have witnessed over the past 40 or more years is a gradual transformation of the core function of finance and banking. Part of this has had to do with a loosening of regulation; part has been a shift toward a transactional business model; part has been the role of technology in widening the distance between bank and customer. This transformational path has in turn led to a growing concentration of financial activity, power, and influence with its attendant risks.

In the provision of financial services, trust is essential. Trust is needed by those who impart their capital to the financial intermediary, and trust is required by those on the receiving end of products and services from the same intermediary. As in any human relationship, trust is a hard-won asset. It can't be quantified. It's an intangible that sits on the balance sheet and its value can only be asserted during times of crisis. As the English philosopher Baroness Onora O'Neill tells us: "Because the public and corporate purposes of banking are deeply linked, it makes sense to think of banking as requiring a social licence … Without a social licence it would be harder, perhaps impossible, to achieve both the corporate and public purposes of banks."[2] That social license is, by design, a fragile construct; it relies heavily on trustworthiness as O'Neill notes. "Trustworthiness is needed throughout personal, institutional and social life, and is both important and demanding in banking, where the activities undertaken are complex and have varied, sometimes very long, time horizons; where they involve many participants but little personal contact; and where much may be at stake and asymmetries of knowledge and skill are common. It is easier to take advantage of others by untrustworthy action in banking than it is in simpler institutions and interactions." If individuals or businesses come to believe that banks and financial intermediaries do not have their best interests in mind, then both trustworthiness, and, over time, the social license, begins to erode. If you were to ask most bankers what is the purpose of the businesses they run, the likely response would be to create shareholder value, putting them in the same category as any other sector of the economy. What's been lost over decades is the sense of distinction between the role of finance and other parts of the economy. If people lose trust in my ability to build safe cars, my company will suffer and, in some cases, people might die as a result. If people lose trust in my ability to safeguard their money, many thousands more will face economic harm should my bank be forced to close its doors. The multiplier effect is many more times that of other sectors of the economy. When the credit intermediation process stops, bad things happen, affecting millions. Ben Bernanke, former chairman of the Federal Reserve, argues in a recent study that while the unwinding of the housing bubble may have precipitated the Great Recession in 2008, it was a "broad-based financial panic, including runs on wholesale funding and indiscriminate fire sales of even non-mortgage credit" that worsened the economic downturn. "The panic in turn choked off credit supply, pushing the economy into a much more severe decline than otherwise would have occurred."[3]

Banks and finance are there to serve the needs of the economy first, shareholders second. If the largest institutions believe the opposite, then their actions, and the climate created in these organizations, are more likely to include behavior at odds with their broader mission and the social license bestowed upon them.

Some observers have argued that what is missing in finance is a clear defined purpose, one that can be measured. Without such a definition, bankers will more easily engage in behavior that is odds with the public interest.

"The point is this: unless it is managed to purpose, the financial system has considerable opportunity to act in ways that are not in the interests of the outside world that it is there to serve," write David Pitt-Watson and Dr. Hari Mann, in a study sponsored by the UK's Pension Insurance Corporation.[4] As we have argued, finance has become increasingly specialized, with technological skills more in demand than before. While specialization may, and should, have benefits to both banks and their clients, it's not clear that's always the case. Pitt-Watson and Mann argue, "while specialisation has benefits, it appears that there are many specialised activities in finance that have no clear value to the outside world. One example would be 'High Frequency Trading' (HFT) … HFT often seems to be a trick to take money from those who trade on exchanges, without their realising it has happened." It would also seem reasonable to expect that over time the business of finance, particularly the role of intermediation has become more efficient. The evidence, however, is startlingly to the opposite. In a recent study by a New York University business school professor, the finance industry has failed to achieve any improvement in productivity for over the past 100 years. "The unit cost of intermediation does not seem to have decreased significantly in recent years, despite advances in information technology and despite changes in the organization of the finance industry," concludes Thomas Philippon in a study that covers the role of finance in the U.S. economy over the last 130 years.[5] The unproductive nature of finance is a topic that has attracted a growing number of researchers. Some have called the growth of finance in the U.S. economy, and its paltry contribution to economic value, "financialization." Rana Foroohar, a journalist who has written extensively on the subject, notes that today's financial sector in the U.S. economy, which includes banks, hedge funds, insurance, and trading houses, represents approximately 7% of the economy's output. Yet, the sector creates only 4% of U.S. jobs, and earns 25% of private sector profits.

"While a healthy financial system is crucial for growth, research by numerous academics as well as institutions like the Bank of International Settlements and the International Monetary Fund shows that when finance gets that big, it starts to suck the economic air out of the room – and in fact, the slower growth effect starts happening when the sector is *half* the size it is today in the US.," writes Foroohar.[6]

In the end, if the activities of financial firms are to do largely with moving money around the world, and creating complex products that increasingly few understand, then the social license given to banks does become questionable. Given the vast number of economic problems facing the U.S. economy—job creation for unskilled workers, crumbling infrastructure, the lack of banking services for poorer parts of the economy, investment in environmental technology, the list can go on—it is hard to imagine that those leading financial firms can't put their effort into activities that drive economic value creation—something you can measure.

The current generation of leaders in finance appears ill-equipped to move their business models back to basics; to simplify rather complicate further. They have grown up in a period that has moved finance further and further from its core mission in the economy. There are growing indications, however, that those coming of electoral age in the United States are beginning to question the role and interests of those in positions of power and authority, whether in government, business or other realms of society. They are asking hard questions, and a common thread through many of them is whether those in charge are serving their own needs, their own interests, or the needs of the many. It's a debate that's likely to intensify in the years ahead, and for finance, will result in uncomfortable conversations for those in current leadership roles. How they respond to questions from a generation that is increasingly restless, and who represent the future, might reshape the narrative over the role of these institutions and their purpose in society. And this is where the link to conduct and culture becomes intertwined with mission. If young people believe they are engaged in activities that make a substantive and lasting contribution to their environment, then that "shared-purpose" will foster the types of behaviors and culture that reinforce one another. If employees are engaged in activities where they can measure and see the value created by their efforts, then there becomes less incentive to engage in behaviors that put clients and their organizations at risk. That is an outcome that all large financial firms should aspire to.

Notes

1. "Facebook to Banks: Give Us Your Data, We'll Give You Our Users," Emily Glazer, Deepa Seetharaman, and AnnaMaria Andriotis, *Wall Street Journal*, August 6, 2018.
2. "What Is Banking for?" Remarks by Baroness Onora O'Neill, Federal Reserve Bank of New York, October 20, 2016.
3. "The Housing Bubble, the Credit Crunch, and the Great Recession: A Reply to Paul Krugman," Ben Bernanke, Brookings Institution, September 21, 2018.
4. "The Purpose of Finance—Why Finance Matters: Building an Industry That Serves Its Customers and Society," David Pitt-Watson and Hari Mann, Pension Insurance Corporation, 2017.
5. "Has the U.S. Finance Industry Become Less Efficient? On the Theory and Measurement of Financial Intermediation," Thomas Philippon, Stern School of Business, New York University, September 2014.
6. "The Economy's Hidden Illness—One Even Trump Failed to Address," Rana Foroohar, November 12, 2016, first published on LinkedIn.

Index

A
ABACUS 20, 25–28, 30, 34, 35, 42
ABACUS 2007-AC1 25, 26
ACA 26
ACA Management LLC 26
AIB Group 88
Alternative for Deutschland (AfD) 61
Alternative Reference Rate Committee 14

B
Bailey, Andrew 49, 51, 58
Banking Standards Board (BSB) 49, 50
Bank for International Settlements 8, 34
Bank of Ireland Group 88
Barclays 10, 11, 15, 16, 35, 56–58
Barrow boys 7
Behavioral economics 5, 6, 60, 62, 65, 67, 83
Behavioral science 5, 9, 58, 67, 69, 72, 73, 82, 83, 85, 88, 92
Berkshire Hathaway 33
Boesky, Ivan 1–4, 6, 21
Buffett, Warren 33, 36
Business Principles and Standards 27

C
Callahan, Patricia 28, 29, 32, 34, 36
CDOs 26, 36
Central Bank of Ireland 88, 89, 92
Chase Manhattan 3
Chemical Bank 3, 4
Citibank 12, 13, 15, 16, 38
Collateralized debt obligations 25, 26
Cottrell, Alison 50
Criminally-based compliance programs 5

F
Fargo, Wells 8, 28–34, 36, 38, 47, 55–57, 72, 87
Federal Reserve Bank of New York 3, 14, 35, 37, 42, 43, 45, 46, 87, 88, 98

Index

Financial Stability Board 53, 58, 87
Foreign exchange market 8, 11, 37, 53, 55
Freeman, Robert 4, 21–23
Friedman, Stephen 21

G
GDR 61
German Democratic Republic 61
Goldman Sachs 1, 4, 8, 20, 21, 23–25, 27, 30, 34–36, 38, 39, 45, 63, 87, 91
Gorman, James 86

H
Hayes, Tom 15, 16, 18

I
Independent directors report 31

K
Kahneman, Daniel 5, 67
KBC Bank Ireland 88
Kerviel, Jerome 53, 58
Kidder Peabody 3, 4, 21

L
Leeson, Nick 52, 58
Libor (London interbank offered rate) 14
Libor rate-fixing 8

M
McWilliams, Carly 13
Merrill Lynch 15–18, 21
Morgan Stanley 39, 86, 87, 92

N
New York State Department of Financial Services (NYDFS) 10, 11, 35

P
Pabon, Alex 15, 16
Paulson & Co. 26
Paulson, John 26
Permanent tsb 88
Prudential Regulation Authority (PRA) 56–58

R
Residential mortgage-backed securities 26
Richman, Ilene 27
Risk arbitrage 1, 2, 4, 21
RMBS 26, 27
Rowland, Derville 89
Rubin, Robert 1, 4, 21

S
Scherf, Molly 47
Snowden, Edward 60
Societe Generale 53, 63
Staatssicherheitsdienst 61
Staley, Jes 56
Stasi 61, 65
Stenfors, Alexis 15, 17, 35, 68
Stimpson, Perry 12, 13
Surveillance state 5, 60

T
Tabor, Timothy 3
Thaler, Richard 5, 6, 83
Thomson Reuters 14, 28, 42, 46, 48, 58, 62, 65, 92
Tolstedt, Carrie 29

Tourre, Fabrice 8, 26
Triennial Central Bank Survey 8, 34
Tversky, Amos 5, 67

U
Ulster Bank Ireland 88

V
Visions and Values 28
von Hayek, Friedrich 3

W
Weinberg, John L. 21
Weinberg, Sidney 20, 21, 25, 52
Whitehead, John 21
Wigton, Richard B. 4

Printed by Printforce, the Netherlands